I0192601

Me 'n Jess
and an Irish Fisherman

Me 'n Jess

and an Irish Fisherman

Patricia A. White

A Paperback version was published in 2010 by Xlibris Corporation.

Me 'n Jess Copyright © 2001
Patricia A. White

Subtitle: "and an Irish Fisherman" added in 2012.

Published by Patricia A. DiVita
High River, Alberta, Canada

All rights reserved. Printing/manufacturing information for this book may be found on the last page. No part of this book may be reproduced or transmitted in any form or by any means, electronic or mechanical, including photocopying, recording, or by and information storage and retrieval system, without permission in writing from the copyright owner.

ISBN- 978-0-9918228-0-5
1. Patricia A. DiVita   2. Pets—Dogs

A portion of the proceeds from the sale of this book or any format in which this books appears is donated to the SPCA. Society for the Prevention of Cruelty to Animals.

Available at:
www.amazon.com/dp/978-0-9918228-0-5

This book is for my sister and my mom.

"You should write a book about that dog."
I heard them say it a hundred times.

Well, here it is. Have fun!

Acknowledgements

Thanks go out to all my family and friends who loved Jesse enough to remember funny stories about her and relay them to me so I could include them in this book. I simply couldn't remember everything she did.

My sister Jenny who so graciously devoted her time and energy into re-reading this book for the third time, to help me edit it, deserves a big round of gratitude and appreciation.

I thank Danny for capturing my heart and making me have to see him again; resulting in my moving to Ireland to write about Jesse.

To my good friend Janet, who shared her enthusiasm for this story about Jesse and kept me motivated to come back to this after many years of shelving it, I say thanks.

To my new friend Steven Johnson who helped me immensely in formatting this book. He taught me what to do and helped when I was frustrated with things like headers and footers. Thanks a mil!

A big thank you to my mom for thinking highly enough of Jesse's escapades to suggest I make a children's book. I'll talk to you later about that Mum...

Jesse. You silly girl. I am so grateful you were the way you were or there wouldn't have been any reason to share you with others. You will always have a big piece of my heart that no dog will ever have.

I still miss you.

Author's Note

"That's MY book! That's MY dog!" It's what I said when I unwrapped the book Janet sent to me: *Marley and Me*.

I have to say something about the book by John Grogan. I am so very grateful to him for proving that a book about an ordinary person and their dog would be of interest to dog owners. When I came back from Ireland, a friend told me that no-one would read my book. "They don't care about you and your dog unless you're Margaret Thatcher or someone." Why he said her, I have no idea, but Marley and John proved him wrong.

I wrote *Me 'n Jess* in 2001 but put it on the proverbial shelf to make a movie about the restaurant industry that I know I was called to make. I made the movie and now it's back to the book.

About *Marley and Me*. The reality is: he was not my dog and that was not my book. The dogs didn't have too much in common and neither do the books. John was married with children and Marley was a boy. I'm single without children and Jesse was a girl.

People read about and loved Marley *despite* his crazy antics. People who knew Jesse loved her *because* of her crazy antics. So yes, our dogs were different, and our books are different. But one thing is absolutely in common. Love.

Foreword

This is the story about my dog Jesse. OK, she never saved my life, or anyone else's for that matter, and she didn't ride a motorcycle or a surfboard, so you never saw her on TV. She wasn't a well-trained service dog with stories of heroics, or a search and rescue dog-- although she could have been one for the Sunbeam bakery if one of their bread trucks was ever missing in action. She was just a dog. But she was a special dog. Ask my friends. They'll tell you. She traveled throughout the United States and Canada with me and saw more places than most people I know, and she was my friend. She was my best friend. She's been gone for four years but she lived a long, healthy and happy life. I'd like to get another dog but I haven't. Guess I'm not quite ready.

I know you're out there...you people with exceptional dogs; you with the perfect dogs. My hat's off to you. Jesse wasn't the perfect dog--not even close--but she was quite a character and we had a relationship I doubt is possible with another dog. I'm not really sure who the master was. She had a mind of her own in a big way. Some of the things she did might surprise you, but keep in mind that Jesse lived for almost 14 years and that's a long time for a big dog. Anyone who has lived with, and loved their own special dog for many years, probably has a whole cupboard full of stories, and I hope when you read these stories about Jesse and her friends, you'll open your cupboard and smile.

I decided to live in Ireland for three months, in order to write the book, so I moved to a tiny fishing and farming village in a northern area of Ireland. The story of this particular place is included, because without the fateful events of my second trip to Ireland, this book probably wouldn't even exist yet. The intertwined story of Ireland involves a handsome Irish fisherman. It was very romantic--full of fate and luck, but this isn't a romance novel; it's real life. So I followed my heart, went to Ireland, and finally embarked on this project.

All of these stories are true. I didn't make anything up. There's sure to be a tangent now and then, but there aren't any tall tales. Jesse provided plenty of stories and fate provided the rest, but I changed the names of the Irish places and people because I wanted to maintain their privacy.

This book might be the type you leave in the bathroom and pick up whenever...I myself don't read at that important time of day. I just don't like it when my legs go numb, or the way my butt conforms to the shape of the toilet seat, and I'm not crazy about getting that red ring across my hamstrings. But you know? A lot of people don't really mind all that. So grab a cup of coffee, get comfortable, and come meet Jesse.

There is a reason why DOG is GOD mirrored.
I think it has to do with unconditional love...

Chapter 1

I want a dog. It's time." I casually made this announcement to the girls, on that cold, rainy, autumn afternoon in Nashville, Tennessee as we sat in warmth and comfort around the dining room table playing cards.

"A dawg at this time of year!? Girl? What are you, nuts? They're a lot of work. Patti you're crazy. You sure you wanna puppy? Poor little thing'll freeze its butt off. Get a pound dawg. Why don't you wait 'til spring? Girl? It's your turn, play the cards." The girls rifled their barrage of rebuttals back at me in pure country twang.

At the time, I was working at Opryland Hotel back when it was little... when it had only five hundred rooms. Nowadays with over three thousand rooms, I'm sure they have to hire long distance runners for the room service jobs. It was a wonderful place to work with loads of fun and friendly folks, and my co-worker-card-playing buddies were as country as they come.

By now I was used to the way Southerners talked. See, I'm a Yankee. It has nothing to do with baseball and it comes from both sides. Southerners call me a Yank and my Canadian family calls me a Yank. Technically I'm a Southerner—born in southern Ontario, but that didn't count with the U.S. Southerners. Being from north of the Mason-Dixon Line; that was it. I was a Yank. Period. And they reminded me of this fact pretty much weekly. I guess some Southerners are still fighting that war from long ago. Oh well, that's OK.

"Well, sure it's almost winter, but there *has* to be a puppy out there somewhere. Ideally I'd want a female golden retriever mix, but I'll find something. I'll get a pup and I'll name her Jesse... Jesse James. Yeah, that's good." I'm not exactly sure how I arrived at that name or why I thought to name my dog before she even existed in my world, but I did. Maybe I felt like an outlaw that day, playing cards in the middle of the afternoon, or maybe it was simply my love of the West. Who knows, but if I had known the outcome of pre-naming a dog, her name would have been Tanya, or Goldie, or Tasha; *anything* but an outlaw name. Self fulfilling prophesies perhaps? I'll never know. But Jesse wasn't a complete outlaw dog—she was in dog jail only twice, however she engaged in many acts over the years that made me question myself; "Why did you name her *Jesse James*? WHY?"

I lived in an apartment at the time, but was moving into a house in a couple of months. I thought I'd feel safer if there was a dog living with me, but not just for protection; for friendship, companionship and just plain fun.

When I was growing up, my family had a great dog named Mindy, so I was used to having a dog around and missed having one at college. The thought of getting a dog when I was in school crossed my mind a few times, especially when I saw all those really cool dogs. You know, the ones with bandanas tied around their collars playing Frisbee. I'd think yeah, I could have a cool dog too. Hey...a guy magnet...yeah. Men know. It's a whole lot easier to approach a woman if she's walking a dog that's smiling and wagging its tail, than if she's walking alone right? But I didn't get a dog. It wasn't fair to have a dog in my life when I wasn't sure where I was going or what I was doing. Yes, I know I'm talking about a dog, but it's a big step. Animals are serious commitments.

Since I was settling down and going to live in a house with a yard, now it was finally time to have a dog.

It just so happens that Debra, one of my card playing buddies, had noticed an ad in the Kroger grocery store for free puppies. She thought they had golden retriever in them, but wasn't sure. So on my way home from the card fest, I stopped at the Kroger and sure enough, it was there. "Free puppies: half white German shepherd, half-golden retriever: call..." Hmmmm...shepherd/golden mix. She'd probably be a smart dog. I'm callin'!

So I hurried home and anxiously dialled the number, hoping they still had puppies. The lady said, "Yes they had female puppies, yes they are adorable, yes they could save me one and they'd be ready to pick up at the end of next week." Yippee! I was thrilled.

"Oh, and one more thing. Their mother died, so we're letting them go at 5 weeks. They're getting to be too much to feed."

"How did she die?" I asked slowly.

"She had mange."

"Oh. What's that?"

"It's a rash on the skin."

"Do the puppies have it?"

"No. We took them all to the vet and he said that the puppies wouldn't get it. They'll have all their shots, so they'll be ready to pick up. Just call next week and we can arrange it."

"So you'll save me a female for sure?"

"Yeah, we have two. Talk to you next week."

"Wait. When were they born? I want to know her exact birthday."

"They were born on Thursday, three and a half weeks ago, it was the twenty eighth."

"Thanks, see you next week." I hung up the phone and danced around the room Snoopy style.

I was really getting a dog! My first dog! All mine... All right! The key word here is first.

If I had been the type of person to fully prepare for having a dog enter into my life, our life together would have been completely different. I would have gone to the bookstore and bought a couple of books about owning and training a dog, and I would have spent the time reading and preparing so I'd have the perfect little dog and I'd be the perfect dog owner; doing everything right because the books say so. I would have known to buy all kinds of chew toys for my little puppy so she could while away those months when her piranha-like teeth would need to be kept entertained, and I would have known ahead of time exactly what you do and don't do to a very young dog and I would have been the picture of readiness.

I wasn't.

But, I know now, owing to some of the mistakes I made because I didn't have the knowledge, Jesse was the way she was in many ways. And if it had been any way, she wouldn't have been nearly as entertaining as she was. If she had been a really rude or dangerous or disobedient and annoying dog, or if she did things that were totally unacceptable to live with, I would have done something different—like shoot her. Just kidding. But she wasn't a bad dog. She was simply a character with some unfix-able habits, and in the end I felt lucky to have had such a wonderful dog. My next dog will be in the encyclopedia under "best trained, most well adjusted, happy-go-lucky, most obedient dog in the universe." Doubt it.

The next week I called and we arranged the day for me to get my new puppy. Friday came and I drove to the house to pick her up. At least I did have a box to put her in for the ride home, so I wasn't completely hopeless as a new dog owner. The ladies' son Mark was there and he took me into the enormously empty three-car garage where they kept the puppies. I heard soft howling echoing from afar and walked to the corner to pick up this tiny white fluff ball of a pup.

"Oh she's so cute," I smiled, and lifted her up very gently.

"Yeah, they were pretty cute pups."

"Hey, I thought there were eight pups. Where are they?"

"Well, some guy came this morning at 6:00 and took all five of her brothers that were left."

"He took FIVE pups?"

"Yeah, he wanted to teach them to hunt. He said they'd be great hunting dogs, and smart too."

"Wow, that's a lot of pups. Oh, so she's been all alone for hours, poor little thing, that's why she's crying."

I held her to my heart and hugged her, speaking softly and trying to console this lonely, abandoned, whimpering puppy. As I held her up to take a good look at her, I exclaimed, "She has crooked eyes!"

"No she doesn't."

"Yes she does, look."

"Well maybe a bit."

Great. I wait all my life to get a dog of my own and she's got crooked eyes. I remember feeling that pit of disappointment in my stomach, but this little one was going to be my dog and that was that. It was too late, in my mind, to change course now. I wanted this pup. (Ends up that her eyes were fine—it was just the puppy membrane.)

So we brought her into the house and while we sat and chatted about the pups, Jesse was crawling around in the kitchen. Psych major that I was, I thought if she wandered around in an atmosphere where she was comfortable and she could hear my voice, maybe she'd get used to it before she was whisked away to a new life. Mark and I visited for a while and I noticed that Jesse was hiding in a cozy bookshelf. She listened as Mark told me that her mother was a purebred white shepherd, and her father (who had jumped the fence) was a purebred golden retriever. She was a purebred half-breed. Perfect.

I've always thought that some of the health problems inherent in certain breeds are weeded out in mixed breeds, and Jesse never had any hip dysplasia problems—common in shepherds and especially in retrievers. We were lucky she avoided this painful condition.

"What about the mange?" I asked Mark. He told me that the vet assured them the pups wouldn't get it.

I eventually headed home with my new little friend in the warm and cozy protective box that she kept trying to leave. I carried her up the steps to the apartment and put her on the floor at the door, and watched as she looked around the room, then slowly and hesitantly put her young nose to the carpet and went snooping around the kitchen, the living room, and into the bedrooms; sniffing at all the new smells and learning the layout of her new home. She was curious about things and didn't run and hide. They say puppy behavior says a lot about what the dog's personality will be like. Is it the pup who continually is hiding and not playing with the others, or is it outgoing and adventuresome? Does it like to be in close quarters, or is it constantly trying to get out of them? So far, she was undecided.

See, I didn't take the luxury of picking out which dog I wanted, by going ahead of time to inspect the litter and choosing my special match. The lady seemed to be in a hurry and I figured, since there were only two females, it wouldn't much matter. I'll never know what that female would have been like, but I suspect that being left alone in the garage for as long as Jesse was would have had the same effect on her. I had no idea if Jesse was the runt or the biggest of the litter, or how she interacted with her brothers and sister, but after she grew up; I figured out that she must have been the Queen Bee. Maybe I would have chosen the female...Nah.

19

Jesse discovered her twin.
She was about seven weeks old.

Chapter 2

Our life together began on a pretty good note, despite the fact that I had to finish weaning her, since she was only five weeks old. Fortunately for both of us, I worked at night for most of my variable schedule, so was able to feed her on a consistent daily routine. I was equipped with evaporated milk that I diluted with water to get the correct nutritional balance, and I made sure she ate her portion of puppy food.

I spent the days playing with Jesse and watching her explore her new home. She did the usual cute puppy behaviors like being completely baffled by the dog in the mirror, or doing the silly-dog-run thing where she'd tuck her tail and zip around the room usually ending up in a tangle of legs, tail and body flying when she misjudged a corner or location of the table. She never really hurt herself, a few bumps maybe, but nothing serious. She was just a rambunctious puppy and she sure provided me with some good laughs.

One evening, I had the night off and was playing with Jesse and enjoying her antics, when my brother Bob called. He had moved to Nashville a couple of months earlier and lived near me in the same apartment complex. I took Jesse to meet him right when I brought her home and he thought she was a cute pup.

"Hey Patti, whatcha doing tonight?"

"Oh nothing, just hanging out."

"You and who."

"No one, I'm by myself."

"You and who?"

"I said, I'm by myself." I replied, slightly annoyed at him.

"You mean you and Jesse, don't you?"

"Oh yeah. Me 'n Jess." I smiled, realizing that he was pointing out the fact that I wasn't alone anymore. My buddy Jesse was with me. And for the next 14 years, she was to be the only constant in my life. Through the few boyfriends, the many moves, losing friends and life's ups and downs, Jesse was there and she was my friend.

They say that people who own pets probably have less stress, might live longer and simply are happier. Sure, sounds great. And coming home to a happy, tail-wagging dog sure beats an empty house. I love cats too, but most cats don't greet you at the door, if they even care to notice that you're home at all. So when your life has taken a dump, talking to a friend who listens and doesn't talk back or judge you, and petting soft fur —even when you can't see through your tears—is oh, so, comforting. When you're feeling all alone, you're not. Your pal is there.

I know everyone's pet is special and different and the relationship between a dog and a person can be as varied as there are stars in the sky. The lady in Florida sporting the flowered dress and gold shoes walking her miniature Yorkshire terrier who is wearing a pink sweater, white booties and yellow ribbons, loves her dog no more or less than the man in Wyoming wearing a cowboy hat driving down the dusty road in the ranch pickup truck with his blue healer sittin' on a bale of hay. Some people treat their pet like a human and others have a working relationship with them. There is no right or wrong. It's just how we chose to, or need to treat our animals. It's personal and it's usually a very loving relationship.

Jesse, however, chose to act like a non-dog dog. She didn't do any dog tricks and she certainly wasn't a working dog. Actually, I was barely able to train her. And I have no idea what it was, but there was a certain quality about her that made her unique. Was it because she was an orphan? Was it because she was abandoned? I didn't know why.

Some of my friends said that Jesse was a person in a dog suit, because she just wasn't dog-like in so many ways. The loyal personality, the obedient behavior, the companionship gene and the desire to please just weren't part of Jesse's make up. She was extremely independent, hardly listened (well, until she was middle aged), and she didn't care what I thought or did. I was merely her entertainment director and not her "dog's best friend". But I know in my heart, she really did love me; she just didn't show it.

She somehow became a dog that people would tell stories about, and many times my friends would come over and see if Jesse could come out and play with them. They'd take her hiking or skiing and leave me behind working. But I was grateful that she was getting exercise and happy that she had such great friends. "Sure, have a good time. Here's a quarter, Jess. Call if you need anything..."

Jill and her blue healer named Kiwi were some of Jesse's friends who took her cross country skiing a lot, and Jill used to say, "You mean Jesse? She's the dog on the verge of words."

Our first Christmas: 1982

Chapter 3

I remember how proud I was the first time Jesse peed on the paper. My apartment was on the third floor and it was winter, so I sure wasn't going to have the time to carry a squirming puppy down the steps to have her pee in the snow, if there would have been anything left after she'd emptied her bladder all over me. Alternative? Paper training. I spread layers of newspaper paper down in the spare room, so she had her very own bathroom.

One day we were romping in the living room, running and rolling around when she stopped dead in her play. She looked up and blinked. It was as if a tiny bell went off inside her little head. She turned and galloped around the corners into her bathroom, squatted her tiny body down, and peed. I was so happy. Yes! She thinks! "Good girl Jesse, what a good girl!"

It wasn't too long before she was potty trained, eventually being able to run down all the steps to go outside, and accidents were few and far between. Too bad it isn't as simple as that for humans.

I was happy that Jesse was potty trained before I went home to Illinois for the Christmas holidays. She was going to stay with Debra while I was away, and I absolutely hated to have to leave her, but at the time, my parents weren't in a position to have a young puppy around the house. Besides, it wouldn't have been fair to drag Jesse along on the 8-9 hour drive. Not to mention the fact that it would have probably been an 89-hour drive, with all the stopping required for a puppy that young in order for her to let out all her energy and pee.

But before I left, me 'n Jess were able to have our first Tennessee Christmas together. Being a fledgling photographer at the time, I had to document the event. I set the tripod up and lit the candles that were beside my beautiful makeshift Christmas tree. It was adorned with popcorn and tinsel and resembled an exquisite candidate for Charlie Brown.

See, I have never to this day had a real Christmas tree. I always went to the tree selling places, gathered the bottoms they had cut off, and tied them together to make a "tree". Sure I could afford a tree, but this was a tradition that started that year.

I discovered the felled evergreens, which had been in the path of future apartment buildings, while I was out walking with Jesse one cold wintry day. It was a terrible waste that they were to just sit there, or be bulldozed into big piles of sad and broken branches, so I hatched the idea of constructing my own little tree. It's a tradition that has provided me with some really interesting Christmas "trees", not to mention some friendly ribbing. My friend Pat claims that I act as if I lived through the Depression with all of my frugal ideas—including my Charlie Brown trees. But my grandma always said, "Waste not, want not, the Good Lord says", and I've been making trees ever since.

OK, back to the photo. So with camera ready and candles lit, I leaned down to pick up my growing white fur ball for our first Christmas photo. As I lifted her up and held her towards the camera, she growled at me! I couldn't believe it. Hey! What happened to the sweet and loving golden retriever personality? I never knew if she just didn't like cameras, or if I had interrupted something very important in her puppy world, but it sure surprised me. I contemplated sending her to bed without opening her presents, but I'm a softy and it was Christmas. As it ends up, one of her bad behaviors would have been avoided if I had done just that. Oh well.

So after the shortened photo session, we opened presents. I still didn't have the training book at this point, or I suppose I probably would have read, "Under NO circumstances should you allow your puppy to open their own presents." Why is this? "Because you are teaching them to rip things apart, dummy." Oh, OK. So that's where I went wrong. I always wondered how she reached pro-shredder status at such an early age, and I finally figured it out...later. But at the time, it was so cute. I softly handed her the very carefully wrapped small package. She took it with her teeth, held it in her paws and started to rip off the paper. She opened it halfway, and then she got so excited that she vigorously shook her head back and forth and backed up around the room trying to free her prize. When she succeeded, I took a picture because she was so proud. It was a small brown rubber Oreo cookie-looking thing that she kept for years, until both the middle and one side were completely gone. Brilliant—buying a chew toy; idiotic—giving it to her wrapped, and watching her rip it open. But it was one of the few toys she had. We didn't have many toys when we were kids; we were always outside playing, so no dog of mine was going to outdo my toy box. Outside with you too. Probably the reason why, in later months, she made both my closet and my housemate's closet her toy box. The shoes...I had...to replace...

Shoulda got the book.

But present-opening wasn't a total fiasco; I did get some adorable photos of the two month old rolly-polly snowball in action.

The day came when I had to pack Jesse up to go to stay with Debra and her large female black lab named Monig. Monig was the one who planted the idea in Jesse's young impressionable mind that it was all right to run around a neighborhood looking for friends or food, and I know that Monig found more friends with food than just friends. It was her favorite pastime and she showed it. Debra would "scold" Monig when she'd come home with barbecue sauce on her collar or Cheetos on her breath, only to be turned right back out to go and find dessert. Oh yeah that works! But she was a good dog and good company for Jesse. Debra assured me that Jesse would be fine and she would take good care of her. So I said my farewells and left for Illinois to go home for the holidays.

Chapter 4

Home for the holidays. We all like to go home for the holidays, right? Sure we do. It's a wonderful time of year. We're all in a great mood, cheerfully shouting holiday greetings to everyone we meet, knowing that we will have time off from work to spend with family and friends, eating everything we want to because the diet tops the list of New Year's resolutions, and wondering what Santa is going to bring us because we were so good last year. Oh wait, I must be on the set of a 1950's movie.

It's not really like that anymore. Stress levels are topped out nowadays. Shopping in crowded shopping centers, the traffic jams, party preparations, cookies to bake, decorations you have to unpack and put up around the house, the lights you have to untangle and hope they work—or go crazy looking for the box of replacement bulbs you know you have somewhere... presents to wrap, cards to write. Whew, never enough time to do it all.

As I write this story, remembering my first Christmas with Jesse, I'm in Ireland, taking a bit of a break from the stress of an American Christmas. Here in Ireland, it really does feel like the set of a 1950's movie. I don't know if it's because I'm in a very small fishing village, or if it's just the way Ireland is. I suspect that it's a little of both.

I'm in Ireland partly because I'm a romantic. And you know? It's tough being a romantic. Life just doesn't behave like those wonderful Nora Roberts or Diana Gabeldon romance novels. Life isn't like those sappy old movies that we romantics watch time and time again—but still need the box of tissues to get us through without salting the popcorn with our tears. No, life is not like a romance novel, but maybe, ever so rarely, you get a moment in your life when there is an adventure such as you find in those novels. This is one of those times.

It started three years ago, in 1997. I was living in Colorado, and my friends B and Z (yeah I know, but that's what we really called them) and I went across the water to Ireland for a horse trek in the beautiful and rugged Connemara and western Ireland areas. It was an outstanding trek with a variety of people from all over the states as well as Germany, Switzerland and Brussels. We had a wonderful time, and I could probably fill pages relating some of the humorous and soap-opera type stories of that adventure, but I won't. Suffice it to say that we still laugh quite heartily about some of the goings on from that trip.

Well, we had so much fun then, that we said to the gang before we left, "Hey, let's do this again in three years, in 2000." Sure, sounds great. We sent out letters to everyone before coming back, hoping to renew some friendships, but sadly, we were the only ones to return. However, this time we brought six girlfriends with us.

It ended up being an almost completely American group (there were two people from Holland), and it was quite an entertaining mix of people from all walks of life and from all over the states. Even though some of these people were the rich and famous types, they all were so incredibly down to earth, fun and a refreshing joy to be around. But we three missed the Europeans because we had enjoyed the fun and the chance to learn about their cultures. I was especially disappointed, because I had been trying to learn some more German so I could tell them something besides der blisteif. Now I could proudly say: der blisteif ist auf dem tish. So not only could I say "the pencil", now I could tell them that, "the pencil is on the table." Not much use on a horse I know, but I was trying.

If you've ever done a "repeat vacation", you have the knowledge that it's never quite the same and sometimes not even close. Well that was the case for the second trek, but it wasn't a bad thing. We still laughed or rode off all the incredible food that we ate and had loads of fun in the process. But it was easier this year to get everyone involved in the conversations, because there weren't any language barriers.

Another main difference was the weather. Last time we were successful in bringing our Colorado sun with us, but this year Ireland took over. We were drenched with rain and whipped by wind on a daily basis, but the rainbows were spectacular—spreading magic right along with the splendid colors.

The Connemara ponies that we rode were amazing animals. Because this year was so wet, we had substantially more boggy land to travel over. I was on a pony for the bogs and loved to watch her choose where she would put her feet. It was puzzling. It all looked exactly the same and she'd be headed in one direction and at the very last minute, change her mind. Then one of the huge Irish drafts would take her original path and they'd sink into the bog. It was awesome how the ponies knew just where to walk. Not that the big horses weren't capable in the bogs, but the Connemara ponies were amazing. Since

31

they're native to the bogs, they learn how to read the vegetation and they excel there. So if you ever plan to go on an Irish horse trek in that area, get a pony for the bogs and a horse for jumping the walls. Either way you're in for a treat.

The events following this year's horse trek are responsible for me being back in Ireland a mere 2 weeks after I returned home. After telling my friends in Colorado what happened, they were pretty curious about the story and amazed that it really happened because it was so romantic and unlikely to happen to me—a confirmed single girl. I tell the whole story later with details, but I want to make it clear that by now Jesse had been gone for 4 years and I had the ability to travel, so I did. The story about going back to Ireland and living there is woven throughout the main story, and involves my girl friends from Colorado and the characters of Ireland, and it was a surprise even to me.

So here I sit in Ireland, looking out to the Irish Sea, soaking up the mist in the air and in my mind, and listening to holiday music as I type.

Chapter 5

My holiday trip during Jesse's first year was shorter than usual, because I wanted to get back to Tennessee and my little pup. I certainly enjoyed the holidays at home, but was surprised to discover how much I missed Jesse. I hadn't had her for long, but she was fun to be around and play with and I really loved her—growl and all. Arriving home late in the evening meant that I had to wait until the next day to gather Jesse and her things. When I saw her, I wondered if she had forgotten me because she didn't seem all that happy to see me. I told myself that she had so much fun with Monig that she just wanted to stay and play. But we headed home and were reacquainted in no time. She had grown in a week and continued to rapidly put on weight. She was healthy and getting stronger and now we could go out walking for greater distances.

Before I left, we had started to get into a routine. We went for walks in the daylight but also for short walks late at night when I returned home from work, and now it was time to extend these walks. It was cold outside—especially at this time of night, but it never seemed to bother Jesse. She had a very thick furry coat to keep her warm. She'd be all excited to go for a walk and we enjoyed the serenity of the evening. No distractions like when we went for our daytime walks. People were always saying, "Oh what a cute puppy! Hi there," as they'd bend to pet her and she'd circle in between and around their legs—tail and body wagging happily. It's not that I didn't want her around people, because as we know, puppies need to be socialized around people as well as dogs, but the quiet of the night was nice.

We walked around the apartment complex and explored all the smells—well, she would explore all the smells; I just walked around smelling the cold crisp air. There was a little tiny hill that she used to tumble down when she was a small tyke because her back legs would be going faster than her front ones, and she'd end up in a tangle at the bottom, but now that she was a "big girl", she'd race down the hill to catch up with me, but often running into my heels and ending up in a tangle anyway.

Returning home from work was great, because now I had company. I had become so accustomed to curling up with a Louis L'Amore book, that it was good for me to get outside and walk in the fresh air. People who work at night generally have to stay up for a few hours to unwind, and now that there was someone to pass the time with, it was more fun to be awake and up and out, before spending time with the characters in the Wild West.

It was while we lived at the apartment complex when I made my big mistake. My fatal error. I broke the cardinal rule of having a dog.

During our walks when she was so young, I'd call Jesse to me and praise her, trying to informally train her to come. Smart. For the most part she'd listen. Well one day, I called her and she wouldn't come. She was too busy poking her nose around in a hole and was completely ignoring me. I shouted her name over and over and over again, but she didn't budge. Finally, she looked up, I called her again, and she walked over to me. I was mad at her because she hadn't listened right away, and continued to ignore me, so I scolded her. Stupid, stupid, stupid.

"Never, ever, ever call your puppy to you and then punish them for coming." I'm sure the book says THAT. I paid for my big mistake for years to come. Honestly, it took her about two years to come to me on a semi-regular basis, and about five to come with a wagging tail. This was the reason why she always tiptoed ever so slowly towards me, watching my every move, if I called her and she even suspected that she was in trouble. Actually, I was glad when she'd even head my way, as opposed to walking off in the opposite direction, looking over her shoulder—giving me the paw. And believe me, she sure was good at that. "Jesse, get over here!" was a very frequently heard statement issued from my mouth.

"Nope, see ya..." was her usual response, especially when she was a teenager, as she happily trotted off into the wild blue yonder. Remember me saying that I made some mistakes with her that molded her personality? Well, that was the main one. She ended up being the Slow As You Go Tiptoe Queen. My neighbor Don used to tell me that his elderly mother loved to watch Jesse walk around the neighborhood in her unique style.

Of course she wasn't supposed to be "walking around the neighborhood" in any style but... And my buddy Pat used to laugh as she described Jesse: "She was a princess, umm hmm, tiptoeing across the street. And the more you'd yell at her, the slower she'd go."

My brother Dave always got such a laugh whenever the three of us were hiking or camping and I wanted Jesse to be with us instead of exploring on her own. He has told me many times: "It always cracked me up when you called her. You'd say, 'C 'mon Jesse. Jesse, come. Jesse, get over here! Jesse! Get over here now. Jesse! I'm serious. Jesse!' Then she'd look at you and go walking the way!" He could barely finish, he'd be giggling so hard.

No, Jesse wasn't very good at the "come" command.

Chapter 6

The day came when we moved into our house. My friend Jim helped me move, and when he saw my new neighborhood, he was angry with me. He was a Southerner through and through, and sometimes they had emotions that didn't make sense to those of us from the North. In words, he was prejudiced. The house that I was so proud to have found was in a predominately Black neighborhood, and that wasn't a good thing in his eyes. (For anyone who insists on being politically correct, I'm sorry, but that was the correct terminology at the time.) I didn't feel the racial statistics were important and of course it ends up that they never were. I made some wonderful friends during the three years I lived there and was sad to leave when I did. It was a great house, with a large yard where I planted a plentiful garden, and there was loads of room for Jesse.

But I wasn't sure where I could let Jesse really stretch her lanky teenage legs, so, many times I took her back to the old apartment complex and let her run around in the woods. Because it was still winter, there was some snow on the ground, and Jesse loved to romp and play in the snow. I'd throw her a stick, she'd run, fetch it, and run back towards me, but she wouldn't stop when she reached me. She'd run right past me, turn, and look at me. "Na na, boo boo, you can't catch me," she seemed to say.

I eventually tried to catch her by diving in the snow, but it was no use. She was quick and thought this was great fun. I figured that she was young and carefree, so I didn't worry too much about this lack of obedient retrieving.

Jesse enjoyed our new living arrangement. Now she had a yard right outside the back door; she didn't have to run down two flights of stairs to go to the bathroom. It was easier for me as well, especially when she had to go in the middle of the night. I'd let her out the door and stand there shivering in the cold, but warmth was much closer and I didn't have to get all bundled up, just to let her out. During this time, I did one smart thing. I kept repeating, "Go to the bathroom Jesse, go to the bathroom," and she eventually learned to go right when she went out, instead of diddling around. That really came in handy when she was older and we traveled all over the country. It saved time when we happened to be in a hurry... she would pee on command.

She was getting older and it was time for me to start seriously training her. My brother Bob suggested that I buy a specific book about training dogs, so off to the store I went and finally got the book. (Since then, I have read more than one book about training dogs, and have seen programs on the Discovery or Animal Planet channels, so my information is from a variety of sources.) Most books talk about choosing the right dog for you and your lifestyle; the right breed, right size, young or old, pound dog or puppy. Some ask if you should even have a dog at all. I've always jokingly said, "People who want children should get a dog first because it really changes your life." It takes time, patience and work to train a puppy— good practice for kids.

Fortunately my free time was in the daylight so I didn't have to train her at night in the dark. UN-fortunately, I was at a disadvantage right from the start. The books talked about different breeds and how you should train this or that particular breed according to their specific characteristics. Remember, Jesse was half golden retriever and half white shepherd. They said both breeds are typically smart dogs and are easily trained, no problem. But when you train a retriever, you should not praise them too much as it will distract them, but you should shower praise on a shepherd, because they need it. Great, now what do I do? I tried the half and half approach. "Good girl Jesse!" to the shepherd, while petting her vigorously. "Well, sort of good girl," to the retriever, looking over my shoulder and not petting her at all. It was a mess.

First I thought I had a dog with crooked eyes; she wasn't. Now I thought I had a dog with a split personality; she was. I could see those canine psychotherapy bills adding up before my eyes. But one thing was plain for me to see. Now I understood her particular version of the fetch game—when she'd retrieve the stick and run right past me. "Here comes the retriever...and there goes the shepherd."

She already knew the "sit" command and now I worked on the "stay" command every day. She was pretty cute the way she'd twist her little head around to watch me walk in slow circles around her. She learned to stay and didn't move her butt at all. I was proud of her the first time I left the room, and she stayed put. I peeked through the doorway and there she sat with a look of confusion on her face. "Mom, where are you? I want to move, but I'm staying, I'm a good girl."

I increased the amount of time I stayed out of her sight and soon, she stayed for quite a while, so I thought she knew and understood the "stay" command pretty well. I later discovered however, that her training in this department was not quite good enough.

We spent the days playing, walking and training. I used a choke collar for the training sessions while trying to teach her to come or heel, and taught her the basic dog commands. As I said before, the come command never fully sank in at that time because I had ruined it, but she tried to behave. I thought it was important to have a decently trained dog who wouldn't be a bother to people, and she was. She had good manners and none of the irritating behaviors; the constant licking, embarrassing sniffing of people's crotches, jumping up at people, or the ball-in-your-face thing that retrievers tend to do. She just missed the "go" part of the "go lay down" command. I guess she was like most dogs who don't want to miss out on any action, so they "go" and lay at your feet.

Jesse's bad habits were more entertaining than anything and she was never injured as a result of them.

Chapter 7

Because our house was old and needed some work (the landlord was all for it), I spent many days painting, wallpapering and building things, like cabinets and shelves. I have to say that last part very loosely, because the shelf I built in the kitchen—to hold all my dishes—came crashing down one night, scaring the you-know-what out of me and breaking almost all of the dishes. Whoops. A carpenter I am not, but I can paint.

Not to give a wrong impression here, but on those days off, when I could work on the house for the whole day, sometimes I'd have a beer. Somehow, painting is more enjoyable when you're sipping a cold Bud. Jesse was great company for me while I worked at home, and she'd hang out with me in the same room. I liked being a dog mom and enjoyed watching Jesse develop into a young lady (she was about five months old by now), but here's where I made another personality-shaping mistake.

I happened to be up on a chair changing a freshly burned out light bulb, having left my beer on the carpet, when Jesse walked up to the can and tipped it over. I heard the strangest sound and looked down to see her lapping up the beer that had spilled, all the while making this really weird moaning, groaning, and humming sound. Luckily, the beer was almost finished, but now she had her paw on top of the can, holding it down, so she could get the last of the cold brew. I hesitated, watching her, then jumped down to get the can away from her. Her tongue kept lapping and I didn't want her to cut herself on the sharp edge.

In the process, I had dropped the hot light bulb on the carpet and now her attention was on the bulb. She went up to it, sniffed it and burned her nose. She jumped back and yelped. Then she started to dance around the light bulb, barking and lying back down, trying to push the bulb around with any part of her face than the tip of her nose. She got mad when she actually touched it again, because it was still hot, but she wouldn't leave it alone. The whole time, the funniest growl came from her throat and a kind of humming sound came through her mouth. Similar to the beer noise, yet slightly different. It reminded me in later years, when Jesse would entertain with her "light bulb trick", of the sound that Mic Dundee made, when he was hypnotizing the water buffalo in the movie "Crocodile Dundee". But add a bizarre bark, a bass hum and a few yips to it—and you've got it. She hated light bulbs for the rest of her life and they didn't even have to be hot. I made sure that she never had the chance to burn her nose again.

As for the beer episode, it managed to turn her into, at times, a true party animal. We lived in a house that wasn't too close to the neighbors' houses, in a relatively central location to the group of friends I hung around, and since I liked to have parties, I did.

"Hey, come on in, good to see you, the keg's over there, cups there, put your coats in there and watch your beer, my dog loves it." This was my usual greeting to guests at every party.

Jesse would go up to any cup within reach, stick her nose in and empty it. If there were cans around, she'd knock them over to get at the beer. She quickly learned that if there wasn't any beer available to her, she just had to ask. She'd walk up to you, sit very straight, and issue her perfected beer bark. It was unlike any bark that ever came from her mouth. It wasn't her usual strong and deep woof. It was a silly yappy, short and choppy sound that could hardly be considered a bark—unless you were a Chihuahua in heat. Her eyes would light up with expectation, her jaw aligned in a goofy grin, and she'd start yipping and yapping away. Then she'd hum while she was lapping up the beer from your hand. And if you didn't pour beer for her right away, she'd edge closer and nudge the cup or can in your hand. There was no doubt what she wanted and she usually got it—that is, unless she was asking her mom and I was cutting her off. People always got such a kick out of the way she behaved at the parties. She loved them. She was quite the social butterfly.

But she didn't need a party for the excuse to have a brewski. Even if there were only two of us hanging out and having a beer, and she was in the mood, she just asked. If it was the first time someone experienced this, they'd ask me, "What the heck is your dog doing?", when she'd sit and look up at them, or usually the beer, and let out this silly bark.

"She wants beer." I'd casually tell them. They'd usually oblige, and after a few gulps, she'd go off and sneeze three times—always three times. She was a hat-trick kind of dog.

Over the years, she even taught a few of her friends to drink beer. Hannah, a low rider black lab, came over one night with her mom Kim, and Jesse had her into the beer in no time.

43

(At Jesse's thirteenth birthday party, Hannah was quite the party girl and had to go home early.) Jesse's buddy Lee Roy, a beautiful pushover of a Rottweiler, learned when he was a pup—thanks to Jesse. He became a master of the art of knocking beer over, spilling it all around and drinking every last drop that left the can. He is currently twelve years old—quite old for a rotty, so maybe beer isn't so bad for pooches after all.

One time I was yelled at by an animal activist—at least that's what I figured she was. She wasn't actually holding a sign or wearing a t-shirt announcing this fact, but... We were at my friend Livie's annual Kentucky Derby party. These were always a grand affair. Mint juleps and all—which I couldn't stomach even after all my years in Tennessee.

Jesse was there with me, carrying on with a bit of beer and enjoying the race. At one point, she asked for another sip of beer and I obliged. It was a party.

"What are you doing?! Giving a dog beer! Don't you know it's really bad for dogs?" the animal activist shouted at me.

"Oh, she loves it."

"It's really bad for dogs." she snipped.

"Hey, she's healthy, and besides, she doesn't drink much, mainly at parties."

"Don't you know that it's really dangerous to give a dog alcohol? You shouldn't be doing that. It's really bad for dogs." she kept on and on—really getting on my nerves.

"Well, she's doing all right so far, she likes beer and she gets it now and then." So there. I abruptly turned on my heel and strolled off to the kitchen to get me 'n Jess another Bud.

So my beer-drinking dog (who, I will remind you, almost reached the age of 14 years old) and I lived in that great house, played in the big yard, and watched as the trees started to bud. The birds returned home from their flight south. Spring was here and the grass turned green.

When the fog cleared.

Chapter 8

Green. Ireland is so green. For the first time in my life, I'm surrounded by green during the holidays, not brown or white. Not only do I see green everywhere I look, I'm in a place named Greenane. You will find it on a map; just remember that I changed all the names and specific locations to preserve my friends' privacy. They're not accurate in a geographical sense, but I maintained the accuracy of the stories themselves. I randomly chose this name because it has "green" in it; to match Ireland's beauty. But the fisherman? His name was Danny.

I'm here indirectly because of a particular castle. It was built in the 1400's to protect against attacks and to try to discourage some of the local families' presence and influence in the area. The first time I was captured by the magic that flows from the ruined walls of the once glorious castle, was when we were walking by, on the way to eat supper.

It was after the second horse trek, and we were tooling around Ireland, seeing wonderful landscapes, meeting friendly people and loving life when we came to this incredible place. I was with my friends B, Z, and Diane, and we were a good combination since we were all country-flavored and agreed on most ideas of where to go and what to see. Z likes to research interesting places to visit, had read about the castle and wanted to see it. So we landed there on this particular Saturday, when they were replaying The All Ireland Senior Football Championship game. It's Gaelic Football, and is equivalent to our Superbowl. But they have a completely different approach to settling a tie. No overtime. Instead, the teams meet again two weeks later on Saturday, then if there is a tie they'll go into overtime to settle the score. Wow. And these guys play just because they love the game—they don't get paid a penny! Can you imagine?

I do most of the driving over there, and I was a bit on the tired side, so I took a nap while the others went to the pub for that oh, so, delicious, Guinness. It had been a process to find a B&B in this small village, but we ended up finding the perfect setting for which to lay our heads. It was an old farmhouse built in the 1800's, situated at the edge of town, overlooking the sea. After my refreshing nap, I walked to town and arrived at pub row. There are two pubs that sandwich a fish-and-chips store, all joined together. I looked through the door that was opened to bring in the fresh sea air, and I saw B inside the pub. I moseyed on in, to find that Sean (the proprietor of the B&B) was there with the girls and there was a lot of laughing going on. So I pulled up a chair, joined in the fun and was slowly waking up to the eye-pleasing Irish scenery inside the pub.

There were Guinness posters everywhere, people drinking Guinness and men who rated a "Guinness". See, while we were in Dublin, before we went on the horse trek, one of the girls came up with a secret code word that would alert us to the fact that there was a good-looking man in the vicinity: "Guinness". If there was a girl at his side, she was a "Harp". I know it's kinda silly, but that's how it is when girls get together on holidays—especially in another country. Always have to keep a keen eye on the boys of different cultures. Research you know. So that was the way we could alert each without inviting suspicion from those around us. Guinness alert; eleven o'clock. And you thought guys were bad about that.

When I first walked through the doorway at O'Malley's, a very handsome tall man with dark hair and smoldering eyes walked closely by me and I thought, "Oh my, a definite Guinness!"

He had resumed sitting at his table by the window and unfortunately, when I took the seat offered to me, my back was to him. I couldn't even take discrete glances at the ruggedly handsome Irish face. However, things do have a way of working out. Sean was trying to tell us about his life in Canada but I couldn't hear him above all the craic (it's Irish lingo for fun and laughter, and even though it's pronounced the same way, it has nothing to do with street corners and money). So it was much easier to hear Sean when I relocated myself to the seat next to him, and of course this relocation had nothing to do with the fact that now I was able to see the strapping young man who was by the window... um hmmm, sure. But, I could also look out the window at the sea and the mist, and just feel the magic hovering nearby. Now I could sneak glimpses of this eye-catching man, and see his wonderful smile when he laughed, watch his handsome face, and observe his animated expressions—successfully doing this discreetly; our eyes never met.

Sean and I started talking about the Greenane area, its history and geography.

I asked him, "What's the body of water out the window?"

"It tis a river."

"That's a river?"

"It tis a river."

"There's no way that it can be a river. You can't even see the side!"

"Aye Patti. Tis a river!"

"But it's too big to be a river. The Mississippi isn't even that big, and it's huge!"

"TIS A REALLY BIG RIVER!"

Case closed. I had a new bantering buddy. (Now, back in Ireland, whenever Sean's making a point, he looks right at me and says, "Tis a really big river." I fully get his meaning, and of course we bust out laughing.)

As Diane and B sat at the bar talking to a group of young fishermen and holding their attention with American tales, Sean, Z and I were discussing the subject of talking to strangers in a social setting and just how to go about it. Z is a shy person, and Sean was explaining the method he used for trying to overcome shyness when he was young. For instance, if he was at a dance, he'd go up to the prettiest girl and talk to her. He said that most men shy away from the pretty girls, assuming that they have a whole string of men already dating them—when that's not usually the case. He would spend hours talking to this girl and he eventually learned to be relaxed with strangers. Interesting method. Makes sense.

I'm not shy. I tend to just go up and talk to almost anyone, almost anytime. I come by that honestly. When we first moved to Chicago from Toronto, my Mom used to drive around and just ask anyone directions to a particular store or special shop, regardless of their gang-like attire, or the fact that they were a bunch of males congregating on the street corner, or that it was a really bad part of town. Yup, I think they thought she was really out there, so it was best not to mess with her at all. Well, she passed that lack of shyness on to me, so walking up to strangers in a social setting has never been a difficult task.

I had bought another pint and was just about to boast, "Well Z, this is how it's done." I was going to walk right over to the man whom I had been watching, plop myself down and say "hi". But I looked over to where he was sitting, and he was gone. Shoot. I had missed my chance to meet him. Darn it. Oh well, that's the way it goes.

Hanging out in the yard by Claude's garden.

Chapter 9

Going back to life in Tennessee, spring had sprung, gardens needed to be planted and we were getting to know our neighbors. Betty and Claude, to be specific. They lived right at the entrance to the community called Hopewell, on the corner of a huge yard, in front of a giant green garden. They were from Woodbury—a small country town southeast of Nashville—and had moved to the Old Hickory area ten years earlier. Jesse and I were downhill from there.

Hopewell was a section of Old Hickory that seemed to be forgotten by time. The houses were old, the people were old, the gardens were big and the pace was very slow. There was basically one way in and one way out, and as you drove further into Hopewell, the houses were still old, but some of the people were younger.

There was a beer joint just down from my house around the bend on the side of the road. It was a swinging place—especially on a Saturday night. I could hear the loud music flowing out the door many a time, but never did go there as it wouldn't have been right. As I mentioned before, Hopewell was a predominantly Black neighborhood, and in those days, there were some places a white woman couldn't go to on a rowdy Saturday night. But a white dog could. Jesse ran around with some of the dogs that lived there, so at times when she got loose, I'd see her passing through the bar yard looking for yummy treats. And she'd get them! She'd come home with a big smile on her face and bones on her breath.

Claude worked at the Central State Hospital for the Insane as a handyman and general helper when patients were unruly. Betty was retired, and unfortunately was in the hospital frequently for various illnesses and ailments when we first moved there, so I saw Claude around more than Betty. When Betty came home from the hospital for periods of time, the four of us spent loads of time together. They were a lovely couple who became like grandparents to me over the years, and I grew to love them dearly. They loved Jesse as their own dog. Even when I visited Claude after Jesse died, I walked into the porch and right there, where all could see, was the photo I had given them when Jesse was a lanky teenager. He loved her too.

Claude wasn't a tall man, but he was as strong as a bull. Whenever I needed help with anything requiring strength, I knew whom to ask. We helped each with projects over the years, especially after I traded in my cancer-ridden Firebird for a Chevy Luv truck. (I hoped to fit in better, in the South, seeing as I had a big dog and a truck. Now all I needed was a gun rack and I'd be in. Maybe.) We used my truck and Claude's ingenuity and strength to bring home the new fridge, washing machine or whatever huge item they needed.

He was shy at first and I had a hard time understanding the thick country accent, and mumbly way of speaking. Swallow your words, don't move your lips and see if anyone can understand you. They won't. But I eventually learned to understand him so I didn't have to just smile and nod whenever I had no idea what he said. He taught me how to cook up a mean mess of turnip greens, a tasty pot of white beans and even a skillet of polk salit. He even showed me where to find it. It grows in the spring, along railroad tracks and fence lines, and only down in the South. Just cook it with some beef roast pieces and salt and pepper, and you'll have a mouth-watering dish if you're a green veggie fan. But be sure to boil it for hours to get the poison out or you won't be around to see how tasty it is. Mmmm mmmm good! Polk Salit Annie sure had the right idea.

After Jesse and I had been living in the house for a couple of months, my friend Gloria moved in with us. We had been roommates in the apartment before Jesse came (hence the mega potty training room). Gloria had decided to move back home for family reasons, but was now ready to be in her own space again. I told her she was welcome to move in with me 'n Jess, so she did. Our adjustment period was short, but Jesse of course had to break Gloria in by chewing a few pairs of her shoes and articles of clothing, and I had to break her in by telling her not to leave bread of any kind anywhere near dog grabbing level. Gloria and Jesse got along great after the initial "breaking in and replacing stuff" period. It was all good and we had a house full of fun.

That summer, my cousin Sandy from Toronto came for a visit. It was the first time she saw Jesse and she thought Jesse was a silly dog. I showed her a few of Jesse's "tricks", like the one with the light bulb, and Jesse showed her how good she was at getting loose. She liked to be in the front yard much more than in the back, and even though her place was in the side yard—the better of both worlds; it still wasn't good enough for Jesse. She bolted out the door every chance she got. Poor Sandy. "Pat, Jesse's out again!"

"That's OK. She's probably just up at Betty and Claude's."

And usually, she was.

Since Jesse was still a young dog who liked to eat things she wasn't supposed to, it made for some interesting stories. To this day, every time Sandy and I talk about Jesse, she brings up what happened one time when we took Jesse to a park to stretch her legs. Sandy and I were sitting at a picnic table while Jesse was roaming around in the vicinity when suddenly we heard this incredible howling. We both turned to see Jesse in the squat position ready to take a poop, but she was walking forward while she was pooping, and kept going faster and faster like she was trying to get away from something while screaming at the top of her lungs.

"Ooow ooow ooow ooow!"

"What the heck is she doing?" Sandy looked at me as I was quickly getting up to go to Jesse. Then she looked back at Jesse and said, "And what the heck is that?"

"I have no idea!" I shouted over my shoulder.

"It's something green!"

I was running towards her now because something was terribly wrong. Jesse was having a hard time getting out whatever it was that was in her, and when I got closer, I still didn't know what it was. But it wasn't good. I gently took hold of this thing and was carefully helping Jesse get rid of it while she was still howling in pain. But I think she knew I was helping her because she let me pull it out. She stopped howling when it was completely out. I let go and it fell to the ground. At first I couldn't tell what the brown and lime green twisted blob was, and then I figured it out. "Oh my gosh Sand!"

"What is it?"

"You're not going to believe it. My underwear. She ate my lime green underwear. So *that's* where they went..."

"Are you serious? She ate your underwear?"

"Oh yeah, Sand. She eats everything."

We still laugh at that story but I always think about the fact that it could have been really bad. That underwear could have caused Jesse a twisted gut and me a big vet bill, or worse, but they didn't. Even when Jesse did some bad things, in the end it was always fine, and many times, pretty funny.

It worked...kinda.

Chapter 10

It was that first summer in Hopewell that it happened. They said it wouldn't. She wouldn't get it. They were sure. But she did. She got it.

Mange.

One day I noticed a spot on the back of her neck that was missing some hair and was very dry, so I took her to the vet. He scraped the area, looked under the microscope and came back in to tell me the bad news.

"Patti, I'm afraid Jesse has mange, and it's not good," he told me in a quiet voice.

"What do you mean 'not good'?" I asked petting my lovely seven-month-old dog.

"Well, there are two types of mange. Sarcoptic and demodectic. They're both caused by mites that bury themselves in the skin and create hair loss. While sarcoptic is extremely irritating and contagious, demodectic is not contagious or irritating, but is almost impossible to cure," he explained.

"So there isn't a cure for the type Jesse has?"

"No, not really. If she had sarcoptic mange, we would treat it with anti-parasitic washes but no, there isn't a cure for demodectic."

"Her mother had mange and they told me that the vet looked at them, and said the puppies wouldn't get it."

"This type of mange is passed through the blood, so the pups would have had the mite passed on to them," he replied shaking his head.

"Guess I should have asked, but I didn't know there were two types of mange. Is there a chance that she'll be OK?" I questioned hopefully.

"Well, no. Once you have it, you have it, but she won't be uncomfortable. She'll slowly lose her hair, and eventually the mite will take over—she probably won't survive. At this time we don't have a cure, but I do know that there is some research going on right now and maybe there will be a breakthrough, so for now, don't do anything rash. No pun intended."

I guess he was trying to cheer me up, but I was saddened by this news and frustrated about the fact that I thought she wouldn't get mange. It's the old "buyer beware" idea and I guess it pertains to animals too; even when they're free or maybe, especially when they're free.

So I took Jesse home and hoped for the best. Over the next weeks her hair started to fall out, but not at a rapid pace. She didn't scratch herself any more than usual and didn't appear to be very uncomfortable. We still went to the lake where she ran around and did everything but swim. She played around as if nothing was wrong with her.

Since the diagnosis of demodectic mange, I knew there wasn't a chance in the world that I'd let Jesse be a mom. I couldn't see taking the risk that this would pass on to any dogs. So I made an appointment to have Jesse spayed. I was very disappointed because she was becoming a beautiful dog with a sweet personality. Obstinate at times—being a teenager, but she would probably have produced a good litter of smart dogs. While she was in for that process, the vet looked at her and wasn't too encouraging, but I still wasn't ready to give up on my little buddy to whom I had become pretty attached. Besides, she still had a substantial amount of soft white hair and was very playful and carefree.

However, the day came when I noticed that all the fur on the tops of her paws by her claws was missing, with the pink skin showing, and her body was losing a lot of hair as well, so I called the vet again. Between the vet bills and the extremely high replacement bills that she managed to create by using Gloria and my closets as her toy boxes from which to pick out shoes and clothes and chew them to smithereens—my free dog was getting pretty expensive. But it didn't matter. I loved her. (Didn't the book say to buy chew toys? Yes, and I did. But she continued finding non-dog things to chew. Remember, it was an old house, it didn't have closet doors, and I still wasn't a carpenter.)

So back to the vet we went and he said it would be for the best; I would have to put her down. Soon. My heart sank.

For all the times when she frustrated me or wasn't the best behaved dog in the world, I still loved her and was so very sad.

I had arranged a trip to visit some friends who lived in Kingsport and I decided on a master plan. I would take Jesse to a vet in that pretty city that's nestled in the upper northeastern corner of Tennessee, and have her put down there. I just couldn't imagine going to her vet here and returning home alone. I'd need time for dealing with this, and the long drive home to Nashville would help.

During the next week, I was an absolute mess at work. I remember that I had to keep excusing myself from my banquet bar to go to the bathroom—to cry my eyes out because I was going to lose my little friend. Living through the anticipation of this upcoming sad event was not easy, but I knew I wouldn't ever let her suffer.

It came time to head east, so we traveled across the marvelous Cumberland Plateau trying to enjoy the scenery. I was looking forward to spending some time with these guys whom I had met a couple of years ago in Florida. When we arrived at their place and they saw Jesse, they were surprised that she was still so playful; looking as splotchy as she did. I told them about my plan and they disagreed.

"You don't have to put 'er down yet. Haven't you tried burnt motor oil 'n sulfur?" one of the guys asked me, sounding incredibly countrified and Southern.

"What? Burnt motor oil and sulfur?" Surely he's not serious, I thought, as I asked in surprise.

"Yeah. You soak 'em in burnt motor oil, mixed with sulfur powder—kills the mange. Didn't you know that?"

"Well, no. I've never heard of that."

"Oh sure. Works 'most every time. The ol' doc up in Bristol always does that to mangy dawgs. They git ther hair back 'n keep on livin. You know mange'll kill 'em if you don't soak 'em," he said, looking very serious.

"Wow! Thanks so much for telling me! I'll soak her when I get home. It really works? Really?"

"Yeah it does."

I didn't want to get as excited about this new information as I did, but I couldn't help it. Maybe there was a chance for Jesse after all. We had a great visit now that I wasn't sad anymore and when I headed back to the big city, Jesse was right along with me in the front of the truck, looking out the window and watching the world go sailing by.

We ran right over to Betty and Claude's house to tell them the good news and see if Claude had any burnt motor oil, figuring that he might—and of course he did. Claude got to thinking and remembered that he had heard somewhere about the oil trick, but he wasn't too sure, so he never mentioned it to me. We figured it was worth a try.

The next day, we brought Jesse out to the side yard, and armed with a gallon of burnt motor oil, a bottle of sulfur powder, a small plastic tub, a pair of rubber gloves and a rope to loosely tie around Jesse's neck, we commenced to coat her with the thick, black, slimy and stinky cure. Betty and Claude helped me to try to contain Jesse in one area so we could avoid getting slimed, and Claude even tried to hold her still whenever her head would twist in the telltale sign of a shake coming on, but she was too quick a couple of times and the black goo went flying all over the three of us. I was so lucky to have such great friends who loved us enough to help with this messy chore and by the end of the ordeal, we were all covered with black oil. I still get a kick out of the photos I took when we were finished. Betty was even smiling in the picture, while black blobs of oil hung from her clothes.

We had used a rope when we were oiling Jesse, but because she chewed through ropes and wasn't at the stage in her life when I could trust her to stay and join in the conversation instead of having to run wild in the neighborhood rounding up her friends, she had to be on a chain when she was outside.

Since it was August—very hot, humid and sticky, poor Jesse was miserable. Covered with the thick unbreathable coat of oil, it was hard to keep her cool. Even though we'd wet her down a few times and re-coat her, she wasn't exactly thrilled with us. She didn't understand what we were doing and she was mad. Of course being covered with a coat of oil meant that she had to stay outside on her chain and one night, I awoke to a loud noise in the sitting room, only to see that she had eaten through the screen to get into the house. Her chain was hanging through the shredded screen, and she was sitting on my beautiful antique couch, smearing oil all over it. I know she wasn't trying to get cool because it was cooler outside. She just wanted to get my attention.

"Hey Mom! Don't you know how miserable I am? Why don't you try being covered in this slime? I'm not a happy camper right now!"

"Shoot Jesse! I know you're unhappy, but it's for your own good."

"Yeah right, Mom. I want to be cool and clean again."

Funny thing is, she was a clean dog. One guy even asked me once if I perfumed her. Yeah sure, if she was a show dog headed for the Grand Nationals, maybe, but of course not— she was a regular dog. But that night she was a regular mad dog. I really felt bad for her, so I took her off the chain and brought her into my room. I put a towel down on the floor for her to lay on, but she started to jump on the bed and I stopped her before she got too far, but the paw print left by the oil was there permanently. (During my last move, I tossed those sheets to the ragbag, but for all those years after that night, seeing that paw print put a smile of gratitude on my face when I remembered the motor oil cure.)

Ends up that it actually wasn't a cure, but it did serve to smother the mites so they couldn't multiply and kill her. After a few weeks of looking like a sewer rat, off to the vet we went for a check up and unbelievably, they had just that week came out with a new dip called Mite-A-Ban. My vet, who was a wonderful man, had been on top of the research. He told me that it was still in the experimental stage and not available for the general public to use. However, he could give it to a special case, but he cautioned me not to expect anything wonderful.

So that afternoon, armed with a hose, a bucket, rubber gloves, the bottle of Mite-A-Ban, a new piece of rope and renewed hope, I started the weekly task of "dipping" Jesse. She still wasn't thrilled in the least and she constantly shook the dip off her fur. We argued the whole time, but at least the water was cooler for her and even though I suspect that the dip irritated her skin a bit, it sure beat the oil routine. I did this for over a month and miracle of miracles, she was cured. The vet was so happy that he had been able to help her and pleased that the new drugs worked. Her hair eventually grew back to an even thicker and more beautiful coat, she forgave us for putting her through such torture and we were happy once again.

Percy Priest Lake

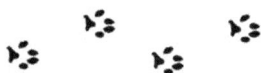

Chapter 11

While Jesse was sporting her beautiful thick white coat, fall finally arrived. No more of the constant sweating, beating bugs off by the millions, restless sleeping in the heat and eating out because it's too darn hot to cook. In the South, most people think that Labor Day means the end of summer; fall is here, take the boats out of the water, it's cold now. I'm Canadian as I mentioned before and that, along with the fact that I was two months premature and had to spend the first part of my life in a hot box like a chicken being hatched, I heat up easily and can really take the cold. I've always wanted to do a study on the incubator and its latent effects on the inhabitant, but never have. But if someone does do that study, I vote that it messes up your internal thermostat.

This was my favorite time of year to go to Percy Priest Lake. It's a very large and lovely lake just outside of Nashville that meanders all the way from Hermitage to Smyrna for 42 miles. The days were still warm but the summer haze was gone, leaving bright blue skies and a good excuse to lie around and read and work on the tan that didn't really need work. The water turned cooler and was refreshing to a sun-baked body when you walked or dove into it. I suppose that people thought I was nuts because I'd swim into late October or even in November if I could, and just loved it.

Jesse, on the hand, would not even get into the water.

She'd rarely get near the shore and when she did, I'd try to coax her in. She didn't want any part of it. I didn't agree with the throw-them-in-and-watch-them-sink-or-swim method, so I let her do her own thing and explore while I swam. I guess I was too easygoing with her, but I got tired of constantly calling her, only to get the over-the-shoulder glance as she trotted happily away. Since we were usually alone at that time of year, no one cared if she ran around or not and we lived in a time before the surge of leash laws.

I enjoyed a relaxing fall, spending my days on the quiet shores of the lake and working nights at the hotel. Fall turned to winter, winter to spring and then, yippee! Summer was here again. Percy Priest, here we come. Jesse was one and a half years old now. Surely, she would swim. She did not.

"All right Jesse, you're old enough to swim now," I calmly told her one day.

"But I don't want to."

"Why not?"

"I just don't want to, Mom."

"But there has to be a reason, Jesse."

"OK. Remember when I was really little and we went walking by the creek and I fell in?" she softly asked.

"Yes, I do, but I scooped you right out before you went floating away."

"Well, it scared me."

"But Jesse, I remember that you went right back in. You didn't seem to care at all," I reminded her.

"Yeah... I know. I was getting something."

"Well?"

"But the water, Mom, the water scared me. It went really fast."

"OK, Jesse. But that was a long time ago."

"I still remember it."

"But it's all right Jesse. This is a lake and the water is calm," I tried to convince her.

"I see that, Mom, but I still don't want to go in and swim."

"You are a dog. You should love to swim." My patience was thinning.

"I don't want to swim."

"BUT YOU'RE A RETRIEVER FOR PETE'S SAKE!"

"Ah, but I'm a shepherd too."

I don't know how she figured that being a shepherd gave her the right to be so embarrassing by not swimming, but she did. She'd still trot off to explore far away from the water's edge and she listened only half the time. Those latent teenage years were pure frustration. But despite these flaws, she was developing into a pretty pleasant dog. I received compliments about her manners all the time, and even though we still argued now and then (mostly about the "come" command), I loved her and had a lot of fun with her. I tried to overlook the "lack of swimming" factor.

There was one day however, when I had had about enough of her bad attitude about listening. She was ignoring me all afternoon, running here and there, flipping me the paw, and I was not in a good mood. My patience was gone. I was completely fed up with her and walked over to get her where she had strolled over to some people who were taking their boat out of the water. She was saying "hi" as she always did—tail wagging rapidly and doing circles like a sideways helicopter blade. She fancied herself to be the welcoming committee of

Percy Priest Lake and got away with it because she was such a friendly dog.

She was ignoring me and wrapping herself around the legs of one of the men. "Hey there, pooch, wow. What a nice dog," he said smiling, as he leaned to pet the soft white fur. "This your dawg?"

"Yeah. She is."

"Gosh, she's really a nice dawg. Beautiful too."

"Yeah." I paused. "You want her?"

"What!"

"I said, do you want her?"

"You can't just give your dawg away like that."

"Oh yes I can. Do you want her?"

"Why, don't you want her?" He was puzzled.

"She's a retriever who doesn't swim. She never comes when I call her and she always..."

"She's young isn't she?"

"Yeah, kinda."

"Well..."

I am so grateful that it was a wise man, who saw through my frustration that day and did not take my dog away from me like I had wanted him to in that short moment of sheer fool-ishness. Later on, it amazed me how I had been heartbroken at the thought of losing her and less than a year later, I was ready to give her away.

Not long after that day when I was temporarily insane, Jesse, my pal Sharon and I went to the lake. Sharon and I were floating around on rafts in the cove, talking girl talk, when out came Jesse, swimming towards us. I fell off the raft. I couldn't believe what I saw. She was swimming gracefully through the water and doing a wonderful job of it I might add. I immedi-ately noticed that her hips were high in the water and a wide strip of her back and her tail were completely above the water, staying dry. She was absolutely a professional swimmer. Well of course, she was, she was a retriever.

"Hi Mom, hi Sharon," she smiled as she cruised by; paws pulling the water strongly and swiftly behind her, creating a lovely wake.

"Oh my gosh, Jesse you're swimming!"

"Yup, and I love it. I don't know why I waited," she grinned up at us.

"You're an excellent swimmer Jesse," I complimented her.

"It's really easy for me mom. Just call me Jesse Spitz." She replied happily, as she sliced expertly through the water.

"You're a silly girl Jesse, but welcome to the water. It's about time."

"Thanks, Mom." She continued to circle around us, before heading to the shallows, where she sat in the water, drinking in the lake and watching us float around on our rafts. Joy of joys, my retriever swims! I always wondered why she changed her mind about swimming, but I was glad that she did, and I never tried to give her away again.

The sheets.

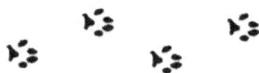

Chapter 12

It was during the time we lived in the house in Hopewell, when I decided that I wanted to try to become a full-time freelance photographer. Already doing photo shoots for some small advertising and graphic companies, I was ready to quit working at the hotel and try to be on my own. I learned photography from books, experimentation, and shooting tons of film. A telephone repairman had taught me how to develop and print black and white film a few years earlier. Merle had come to fix the phone. He saw some of my shots on the wall, asked who the photographer was, and later taught me to process film. Eventually I bought an enlarger and darkroom equipment and stayed fairly busy with a small business. I was lucky. I didn't spend big bucks on university courses like Sharon.

Sharon was enrolled at Middle Tennessee State University in Murfreesboro for photojournalism and she also taught me some photography techniques for which I was very grateful. One day we spent the day at school and apparently we were there too long. When I returned home, I found that Jesse had eaten a big hole in the backrest of my beautiful antique couch

—the one that had eventually recovered from the oil episode. I was furious with her and yelled at her as I shoved her out the door into the back yard.

"You ate my couch! I can't believe you ate a hole in my couch! Why did you eat a hole in my couch?" I screamed at her through the open door. Oh, I was mad at her.

They say, dogs don't actually get mad at their owners, but are bored or just teething or whatever; yeah, right. They get mad, period. I bet dog owners would agree with me and can remember destruction caused by their angry canine whom they left alone one too many times. Well, I guess that I hadn't been spending enough time with her while trying to start a business, so maybe that was the reason for her anger. I know she didn't have a full bladder, because she didn't immediately squat and pee—I was watching while I was yelling.

Yes, I know you have to catch them in the act and yell at them then, in order to do any good in the learning department, but I was furious. I didn't hit her or else bones would have been flying all over the place, and I don't mean milk bones. I was that mad and she knew it. She had ruined my gorgeous cherry wood antique couch that a dear friend had given to me, just because she was upset.

I covered the hole with a large antique doily and lucky for me it was the only furniture she wrecked, because I was gone a lot during those days. I went to advertising agencies, record companies and graphic artists, showing them my portfolio and trying to get work. I usually left her inside when I thought she had bothered Betty and Claude enough for the week. But if I left her outside, invariably she was at their house when I returned. One day I went up there.

"Hi you guys, how was your day? Jesse here again I see."

74

"Well, she was howling and getting all twisted around the shade tree, so I brought her up here," Claude was making excuses for her again.

"I hope you don't mind having her," I asked them, darn well knowing the answer. (They just loved her company, as they didn't have a dog of their own yet—they got one after we moved.)

"Oh no, not at all, we love her, Patti." Betty said smiling brightly, looking up at me from her usual seat at the silver legged kitchen table in their tiny little linoleum kitchen.

"Good, I'm gla... Betty? Why are there Spaghettios in a dish on the floor?"

"Hmmm?"

"There's a dish, on the floor, that has Spaghettios in it."

"Oh." Betty rolled her eyes and sheepishly said sideways, "Guess she didn't eat them all," as she looked to Claude for support. Then Claude went into some long and drawn out story about dogs on the farm and their curious eating habits. Umm hmmm. Right.

Even though I really tried not to give Jesse too much people food (she usually helped herself when she grew bigger and could reach the counter), I just couldn't be mad at Betty and Claude when they fed her leftovers, which they did on a regular basis. She ate better than I did during those difficult stretches of waiting to be paid from photography jobs.

Well, that's not exactly true. Jesse and I both ate pretty well at B&C's diner, as I sometimes thought of the little white sided house next door. I rarely went over for a visit without them feeding me. I must have looked pathetic or something, because no matter how hard I tried to convince them that I had eaten, they'd shove a plate of turnip greens, white beans and corn-bread in front of me and I had to eat it all. I couldn't complain and have to admit that they were the best vittles you'd find any-where, including all the thousands of country restaurants in Tennessee. I wasn't much for cornbread, but Claude would put mayonnaise in it and it was yummy. Try mayo in meatloaf too, it moistens it right up. Claude had learned cooking from his sis-ters who grew up in the back hills of Tennessee and anyone who has enjoyed the pleasures of down home cooking in the South, would know why I was always happy to oblige those two loving folks who wanted to keep us fed.

Chapter 13

We needed food on that Saturday evening back in Ireland. We eventually left the pub and walked down the dark road on our way to the historic restaurant next to the castle. We were laughing and carrying on, and as we strolled by the castle, I glanced over and saw a sight that stopped me dead in my tracks. Moonbeams were softly illuminating the stones that were once the majestic castle walls, while the moonlight was outlining the crumbled ivy covered towers and fingers of remaining stone as they reached softly into the sky. The moon was reflected on the water of the sea as it shimmered in a billion points of light just beyond the shoreline. It created an amazing aura of enchantment and was a magical scene that I will never forget as long as I live. I stood there staring at the mystical view before my eyes.

"Oh my gosh. You guys! Come here! You have to see this." I shouted to Sean and the girls.

"Patti, what are you doing? We're hungry."

"I know, but you have to see this. I mean it, come here."

Diane enjoyed photography too and was the only one who walked back to witness this exact sight. I told her to cup her hands, look through and imagine what an incredible photo it would make. As she did this, she wholeheartedly agreed and we stood there, gazing at this wondrous picture.

We ran to catch up with the others and continued on only to find out that the restaurant was having a private party, so we headed to Duffy's Inn for a scrumptious meal. I was continually amazed at the prices we encountered in Ireland for the quality and quantity of the food we ate. My meal of a good-sized fillet of blackened red fish, accompanied by three crab claws, three large prawns, vegetables and potatoes, was only nine punts and it was delicious. By the way, punts are Irish pounds and were equivalent to just over an American dollar at the time.

So after filling our bellies with great food, B, Z and I decided to go back for a pint before retiring after a fun Irish day. We had been typical tourists: driving around the wet countryside, spending time in a quaint Irish pub and meeting the locals.

We walked into O'Malley's pub, looked around, and who was sitting at the corner of the bar right in front of me? Him. That guy. Oh my gosh. I walked up next to him, ordered pints for the girls and myself, turned to him and said, "Hi, you're back."

He shyly said yes and then mumbled something to me that I couldn't understand (fisherman's style I found out later), but I sat down next to him anyway. Z and B went to sit at a table, but I wasn't budging from my seat next to this handsome Irish man. "Hi, my name's Patti, what's yours?"

He introduced himself. His name was Danny. He wondered how we ended up there so I told him about our holiday and how it happened, and then we started talking about fishing in Ireland, life in the mountains of Colorado and anything else we could think of. Even though I had to continually ask him to slow down or repeat himself, conversation came easily for both of us and I was content to be sitting so close to this intriguing man. I was charmed by his beautiful smoky green eyes, his wonderful smile and casual manner. Not only was his lilting Irish accent alluring and his face easy to admire, his conversation was interesting too. I enjoyed hearing about his fisherman's lifestyle and listening to stories about being at sea. We sat and answered each 's questions about our very different lives, laughed together and learned about each .

Danny's buddy Ryan had joined in the conversation, so Z pulled up a seat at the bar and tried to help me figure out what these fishermen were saying through their non-moving mouths. It was futile. I feel sorry for someone who reads lips and comes here for a visit. They wouldn't have a chance...not a chance. I think that over time the boys finally grew tired of repeating everything, so they slowed down when they were talking to us, but when they'd talk to each , we couldn't understand a word.

Eventually I became better at interpreting his accent and I learned more about this man who had earlier captured my attention from a distance. Happy to be up close, talking, looking, listening for hours and being intrigued by his stories, I was finding it easy to be comfortable with him. When Z wanted to go, I wasn't leaving yet and after saying bye to her, I continued to find out more about life in Greenane.

So on that Saturday evening, my "one pint" idea failed. I sat and talked to Danny and his friends into the wee hours of the morning until it was really late and time to go. I said something to Danny about walking me home and out the door we went— to a jeer from the boys in the back. We crossed the street and headed towards the shore path, where I could hear the waves softly lapping the shore.

When we reached the path, he stopped. He slowly turned me towards him and silently leaned down and kissed me. My heart leaped, I caught my breath and my knees gave way. If his strong arms hadn't been embracing me and holding me up, I would have been a puddle on the pavement. I literally melted into the embrace and for a moment, I lost all sense of reality. Or maybe I lost all sense of fantasy. I was standing by the Irish Sea, with the soft wind blowing and I was kissing this incredibly sexy Irish fisherman. What's going on here? I know we read those romance novels that talk about being weak at the knees, but it really happened.

You're probably thinking oh sure, you had been at the pub all night, no wonder your knees buckled. Well, some hours earlier, after a few pints, I had switched to drinking water. I knew that I was going to have to drive all day on Sunday and since I had previously experienced having a fogged head while driving on the side of the road, no thanks, not again. Not if I could help it. Yet, I wasn't going leave and miss out on the fun or the time I could spend talking with Danny and getting to know him. So, this weakening of the knees had nothing to do with the pub and everything to do with this Irish fisherman who was causing my pulse to race.

After we slowly and reluctantly released the embrace that had a hold of more than my body, we continued walking along the path next to the sea. Between the soft waves, the sweet scent of the salt water and the closeness of this dashing man, I was held in the soft hands of a romantic cloud. Now when he talked, I could understand everything he was saying because he spoke softly and slowly to me. I loved just listening to him speak.

We continued walking and stopped at a grassy knoll. As we sat and looked out at the water that shimmered in the moonlight, we talked some more about fishing in Ireland and life in the mountains of Colorado. Our conversation was stalled by occasional kisses and strong hugs, but somehow we managed to learn more about each 's lives. I was stunned that I could feel so strongly about this man whom I barely knew. He had completely captured my heart and my mind was letting it happen. When he stood and reached to help me stand, I looked up to see his face silhouetted against a dark sky that was dotted with the light from a million stars, and I heard his soft Irish accent in my ears. I hugged him and kissed him, feeling his strong arms around me—holding me, and while this was happening, I became that "American girl in Ireland". The one whom you read about in a Nora Roberts novel. I couldn't believe that it was happening to me. To me! It was almost more than I could bear. It was a moment in my life that I will never, ever, forget. Just breathe...

It was quite late when we reached the B&B, because we walked slowly down the dark and silent country road and we stopped frequently. We sat together for a long time before I had to reluctantly send him on his way. It was extremely difficult to say good-bye. I wanted to spend so much more time with him and get to know this quiet Irish man. We tried to go our separate ways, but repeatedly came together to hold each and kiss our last kiss. I asked if I could call or write or something, but he told me that he wasn't reachable. After one last lingering kiss, I watched him walk down the stone walkway towards the road. He turned and raised his arm in a single wave. I thought as I waved back to him, that I would never ever see him again. There was an unexplainable feeling in my heart and I felt incredibly empty and sad.

Taking a chance.

Chapter 14

I was saddened when our landlord told Gloria and me that we had to move. Her son was moving into the house and we had to move out. I was really going to miss Betty and Claude, but I made sure that Jesse and I went to visit as much as we could. I found a duplex just a few miles from Hopewell, in the village of Old Hickory, and moved in with my friend Gina. She was a girl whom I had met at the Penalty Box; a pool bar in Hermitage that I occasionally visited. It was owned by the brother of an ex-Blackhawk hockey player, hence the name, and it was a fun place to bend an arm, as well as shoot pool.

It was while we lived in this house that Jesse pulled one of her best counter food thefts. I had stopped at the store around the corner and picked up a beautiful fillet of cod for a late dinner. I set it in an oven-ready dish on the counter and was in the process of making the butter sauce, when I realized that I didn't have quite enough butter. I pushed the dish with the fish way back on the counter and headed back to the store around the corner.

"Weren't you just here?" the check out gal asked.

"Yeah, but I got home and realized that I needed more butter." I smiled as I paid and then strolled out the door with my bag. My mouth was watering at the thought of the butter sauce draped over my fillet. I arrived home and went into the kitchen that was about the size of a janitor closet in high school and was unwrapping the butter when the phone rang. While my shoulder tucked the phone against my ear, I stood at the stove chatting away and making my butter sauce. I turned to retrieve my fillet and the dish was fish-less.

"JESSE!" I shouted into the mouthpiece. I gritted my teeth and calmly apologized to my friend, whose ear I had just blown off. "Sorry, can I call you back?"

"Why, what's wrong?"

"Jesse... ate... my fish."

"What?"

"Jesse. Ate. My. Fish. The one I was going to eat for dinner." I was so mad that I could hardly get the words out of my mouth. "I'll call you back OK?"

I hung up the phone and picked up the empty dish, staring at it, hoping the fish would magically appear. I couldn't believe she ate my fish. She had never eaten fish before and it was all the way in the corner. How did she reach it? It was a small kitchen, but still! I yelled at her again and before I smacked her in frustration, I shoved her outside without hitting her. I actually wanted to break the dish on her head! Not that I'm prone to violence, but once again Jesse's action triggered my Irish temper and I made her leave the area before I reacted. Then it suddenly occurred to me that she had been hiding behind the dining room table when I came home, and though I thought nothing of it then, now I knew why. She was a thief, but she didn't brag about her thievery. She was just a sneak.

So back to the store I went. You know how it is when you have a taste for some certain type of food and you have to have it. Besides, I had the sauce. I found another fillet, but it wasn't cod, they were out of cod. Delightful. I went to pay and the same gal silently gave me a look of bewilderment.

"Jesse ate my fish." I pouted. (The whole staff at Food Town knew Jesse.)

"She did?"

"Yup."

"Where was it?"

"On the counter, in the corner."

"How'd she get it?"

"Beats me, but she did." Needless to say, I was very hungry when I returned home from my third trip to the store. And with my fish held high so Jesse couldn't even get a sniff at the bag, I went inside and prepared my supper. She stayed outside while I enjoyed my fish dish; alone.

Gina's folks had a wonderful farm in Hermitage where she kept her horses and donkey. Jesse and I would go out to the farm any chance we could. It was a pleasant and peaceful place and we both loved it. I don't know how she first figured it out, but whenever we headed down a particular road and could only be on the way to the farm, Jesse would start running back and forth in the bed of the truck, vigorously wagging her tail and happily moaning loudly. I'd ask her, "Where are we going Jesse, are we going to the farm?" She would always know.

They say, dogs don't really remember places by sight or familiarity. They see a motion you consistently do and become conditioned to know what is going to happen, but I don't believe it for a moment. They know. They remember. If you've ever had a dog, you probably know this too. Jesse would always know when she was going to see her friends on the farm. Monroe the donkey and Jesse had a love-hate relationship. Jesse loved to play with him and chase him around, and he hated when he couldn't catch her to stomp on her.

Jesse had a rare moment of behaving like a bona-fide retriever one day at the farm. My Kingsport friends were visiting us, happy to see that Jesse was so healthy now, and we went to the farm. They were golfers and had their clubs with them, as I guess most golfers always do. I don't know. I don't golf. But that day I had a brief encounter with the intense sensitivity that golfers must experience when they're holding a golf club. I swear I could feel the earthworms breathe when I was teeing up the ball. It was amazing. I was so conscious of every movement I made while getting ready to send the ball sailing into the wild blue yonder: adjusting my weight, checking my grip, squaring my shoulders, focusing on the little white spot on the ground, asking the crowd for silence and swinging the golf club. Mind you, my ball never got off the ground. It headed in a perfectly straight line into a pile of leaves that were about fifty or so yards away: every, single, time. The best part was that Jesse thought it was a great game. She had so much fun rummaging in the pile of leaves for the ball, scooting here and there with her nose to the ground, sniffing for the ball. And when she found it, she'd do that retriever get-a-better-grip-on-the-ball-head-toss-thing, come running back to me, and drop the ball at my feet. What a gal huh? My little retriever...

Another summer afternoon, Gina and I planned to meet at the farm to fly kites and practice shooting rifles. No, I didn't have a gun rack yet, but I was trying to be a Southerner by practicing anyway. In the late morning I had an appointment to see an artist to show him my portfolio, and since it was more convenient for me not to go home to get Jesse, I brought her with me.

Unfortunately she had developed the bad and potentially dangerous behavior of occasionally jumping out of the truck when she was supposed to stay. (Remember the "stay" command deficit?) I couldn't leave her inside the cab—she'd die of heat stroke—so before I headed up to the meeting, I begged her to stay in the truck. She assured me that she would stay— with one of those "Sure I'll listen Mom." looks, but I soon found out she was fibbing.

I was in the middle of my portfolio presentation when I heard, "Hey there big fella, what's your name?"

I turned quickly, just in time to see Jesse's big white wagging tail disappear behind the doorjamb of the lawyer's office next door. Jesse! How in the world did she get up here? Well...she went through two doors, climbed two flights of stairs, passed through another door, went up a short flight of steps and around a corner. Great...now she's a bloodhound! The graphic artist decided the appointment was over. I red faced excused myself, quickly gathered my things, and grabbed Jesse while profusely apologizing to the lawyer who stood in his beautifully decorated office smiling and petting her, then I slithered out and headed down to the truck with Jesse in tow. I never could reschedule with that artist for some reason. Maybe he had a cat.

I was furious with Jesse as I loaded her into the truck and had half a mind not to take her to the farm, but those were the days before everyone and their grandmother had a cellular phone, so I had no way of letting Gina know if the plans had changed. When we arrived, Gina was already there tying tails on the kites and setting up the rifles. We took advantage of the warm breeze and had fun flying the kites and watching them dive-bomb into the tall trees to spend eternity there, then we fired off a few rounds with the rifles. Jesse was doing a really good job of ignoring me and wouldn't move out of the way while we were shooting, so at one point, I shot at her. Well, I should say that I shot at the ground way in front of her, and boy did she jump! She got the message and stayed over to the side while we carried on. That's partly why I don't have a gun to this day. I'd end up getting so fed up with her antics that I would shoot my own dog. Not really. Maybe I just had an issue with disobedience.

Gina had a female black lab mix named Shadow. She and Jesse were good friends and they hung out with the landlords' mutt Toby, who shared the yard of the duplex. They were a mischievous trio. They all played together in the yard, and one day I caught Toby red-pawed with one of my cowboy boots, well, what was left of it, so it's not like he was an angel.

I wasn't sure if it was the fact that Shadow decided to have a large litter of pups one day (she chose to start the process on my antique couch—that poor couch), or if it was when the dogs decided to dig an entire network of tunnels to China that even the men of Stalag 13 would have been proud of, but the result was: Jesse and Shadow got the boot. Toby sat at the gate snickering when the girls left.

Due to my work and football-watching schedule that I had planned for that weekend, I asked the landlords if I could bring Jesse back to the house for a while on Saturday and they said "yes". They really were a nice, sweet young couple and I understood about the dogs. Gina was going to be gone, so I figured it was all right. Well, Gina happened to come home, and when she saw Jesse there, she figured she should bring Shadow back too. Then the landlords saw Shadow, and now we all got the boot. The lesson? You should always ask.

Now I was in a dilemma. I had to find another place to live that allowed dogs, and find it quickly. Plus, now I was on my own as Gina wasn't talking to me to say the least. I never really figured that part out. But once again, the Good Lord smiled down on me. My friend Belinda asked her mom Joyce, if I could move in with her until I found something else. She said yes, I could, but Jesse couldn't. Betty and Claude. Help! They did. Jesse moved in with them and I moved in with Joyce on a temporary basis—the one and a half year plan.

Joyce took this in front of her house.

Chapter 15

After we moved, I was working a lot, but I planned to go see Jesse every Tuesday afternoon and Saturday mornings at the very least. I was very grateful to Betty and Claude for keeping Jesse for those few months, and since I didn't want them to think I didn't trust them, I let them enjoy her without me constantly coming over and bothering them.

Betty told me that Jesse always knew when it was Tuesday and Saturday because she'd sit at the window and watch for my truck. I'm sure Jesse would be mad at Betty for telling me that, because after a quick wag of the tail and head up for a pat, she'd go and sit right next to Betty or Claude and pout—not even looking at me. I'd go over and lay down next to her to pet her and talk to her, but she wasn't talking to me at all. I felt like a terrible mom, having her live away from me, but knew that she had Betty and Claude wrapped around her paw.

On those visits, I made a point of not looking at the bowl on the floor to see what treats Jesse was receiving from Betty. I was an absent parent. Those two loved having Jesse around and she was a bright spot in their lives; giving them someone else to talk to and someone to spoil. Betty told me how she always had to get up at six a.m. to let Jesse out to go to the bathroom. I told Betty that Jesse didn't have to get up then—she never did with me. She was just getting more attention from Betty because she knew she could.

"Oh no", Betty would say, "She really has to go."

Well if you want to get up at that time of day to let her out, fine, but I sure didn't. I raised Jesse on a night person's schedule, so that stare-at-you-over-the-edge-of-the-bed trick that dogs love to do, didn't work on me—unless of course I knew that she really had to go out, in which case she'd tell me. I was on to her morning tricks with Betty, but I never convinced Betty of that.

I really missed having Jesse live with me, but I was a little nervous about asking Joyce if we could have her, so it was about three months later when I rounded up enough courage to ask Joyce about Jesse. She agreed to have her, but only outside. So we put up a fence to keep Jesse confined. It didn't work. And for some reason, Jesse chose to jump the fence at some of the most inopportune moments. One time, Joyce's daughter Melissa was at the house when Jesse disappeared. Melissa drove all around the neighborhood and Joyce scoured the streets. Both were frantically looking everywhere for Jesse. They finally gave up.

"Patti, we were worried sick. Then, here come Jesse, up through the field, just a slidin' on her belly." Joyce told me. They were relieved to say the least, even though they both just wanted to strangle her.

Joyce would remind me of Jesse's bad habit when I'd go and visit her in later times. "If she could get away, she was off like a blue bullet, gone in a heartbeat. Ain't no use in trying to catch her. I just always said, 'Jesse, please don't get killed, your Mama would kill me!' "

92

I assured Joyce that wasn't true. I knew who was to blame.

Since keeping Joyce in a constant state of worry about Jesse's escapades wasn't a nice idea, I had to put Jesse on a chain by her doghouse. So I made a point of taking her out on excursions as much as I could, and we still went to Percy Priest Lake quite a bit. Yes, she was a real water dog by now and I even taught her to take me to shore. I'd lie very straight in the water, floating right on the surface, being as buoyant as possible and I'd gently hold on to her tail (near the base) as she'd pull me around, happily swimming like a furry white tugboat. I didn't think about it at the time, but teaching her to take me to shore was a smart thing to do. If I ever cramped up in the water and couldn't swim, I had my rescue dog nearby.

One afternoon we went to a different spot than the one we normally frequented—just for a change of pace. I was lying by the water after a good long swim with Jesse and a couple of her versions of fetch.

Unfortunately Percy Priest wasn't the cleanest of lakes at the time, so sometimes she'd find a can floating around, and after bringing it to me for a few tosses, she'd swim away with it. I guess recycling wasn't in her program either. I did manage to take some of the cans home with me, but not all of them. I never knew when she'd come back or not, so I could take the can from her, but after Jesse had bitten holes in them and let them go, I guess they filled with water and sunk to the bottom of the lake. This wasn't an everyday thing and I'm sure she wasn't the only one contributing to the beer can graveyard. At least she was cleaning up the surface of the lake.

Anyway, I set out to catch some warm sunrays, and since nowadays Jesse usually stayed fairly close to the area where I sunbathed, I was content to read and then take a catnap. I had noticed earlier that there were a few guys playing Frisbee in the water, and they were later joined by a couple of guys who were having a beer and a good time, and I really didn't think too much about it. Before my nap, there were five guys in the vicinity. After my nap, I awoke to about twenty guys laughing and carrying on. I immediately felt very out of place and sat up thinking, "Where's Jesse?" I quickly put a shirt on and walked up towards the picnic shelter to find another mass of men having a good time. I discovered that a fraternity from Vanderbilt was having their annual lake bash, and Jesse and I were in the middle of their party. Actually it was Jesse who was in the middle, and she was being a real party animal yet once again.

I walked over to her and asked, "Jesse, what are you doing?"

She looked up at me and smiled as the young man standing next to her asked, "Hey, is this your dawg?"

"Yeah, she's my dog. I hope she's not bothering you."

"Oh, heck no. She's a real cool dawg. Her name's Jesse?"

"Yeah..." I answered him, wondering why he thought she was cool.

"Man, she loves beer!"

"Yes, she certainly does. And how did you find this out?" I asked as I gave Jesse a very stern motherly look, while laughing on the inside because I knew exactly how he had discovered this fact.

"Well, she come walking over and I pet 'er 'cause she seemed real friendly, then she started acting strange, kinda dancin' on her paws, and barkin' this weird bark."

"Yeah?"

"Then, when I leaned down, she put 'er nose on my beer can. I figured she wanted some beer, so I gave 'er some."

By this time, a few more guys had gathered around, asking about Jesse and saying what a great dog she was. Apparently, while I was napping, Jesse had become an honorary member of this fraternity by impressing the boys with her beer-drinking skills and talents.

"Hey, she's an expert at catchin' Doritos. She's really good at it. I even tossed them to her from far away and she never missed!" piped up another of the guys.

"Well, she's a popcorn pro. We practice all the time, so I'm not surprised." I told him, not sure if I should be proud of her catching abilities or embarrassed that she could be such a beggar.

"She had a hamburger too. It fell on the ground and she scooped it right up, hope that's OK," another guy threw in.

"Oh she did, did she? Yeah that's OK. I just hope she wasn't a pig. She can really be a mooch." I was sure she had more than her share of the boys' beer and food.

"No, she's a great dawg!"

"Hey, she's fun to have around."

"We love watchin' her drink beer and then sneeze!" The guys told me with big smiles on their faces. Jesse was having a wonderful time with her new-found friends who would feed her anything she wanted, and since I didn't want to be a stick in the mud and spoil the fun, we hung out with them for a while. But I did cut her off from the food trough. I honestly think they would have liked to have taken her home and made her their new mascot for their frat house.

Had they known about one of her bad habits that came to show its ugly face another summer day, they would have changed their minds. My pal from Illinois was passing through Tennessee while deciding what to do with her life, and we were at the lake with Jesse. Kelly and I were soaking up the rays and figuring out the world's problems, and the fact that she should stay with us until she knew what she wanted to do, when I noticed that I hadn't seen Jesse for a while.

"Where's Jesse?" I stood up to go and look for her, when I saw her emerge from the trees carrying a large, long and dark tree branch-looking thing. She was still about forty yards away when the stench of this thing hit us like a slap in the face with a dead fish.

"Oh my gosh Kelly, what the heck is that?!" I shouted through my hands that were covering my nose and my mouth.

She hadn't turned around yet but answered, "I don't know but IT IS RANK!"

"Jesse, what are you doing and what the heck is that?" I said to her as she drew closer. Feeling sick because it looked like a bone, I suddenly thought it was a human body part and my stomach lurched. I could hardly stand there. The smell was so incredibly strong and foul.

She pranced right by me, still barely talking to me—because she was living in the doghouse and not in the people house—and she headed towards the water. I stepped closer to her to try to get a better look at this pungent grotesque thing without keeling over; thinking and hoping, "surely it's not human".

"It's a leg of some kind." Kelly observed, while holding her nose and turning blue.

"No way, you think?"

"Yeah, look at it, it bends and that's a bone there, see it?"

"Oh man, you're right. It's from something big I think. Jeeze, I thought at first it was a human body part, but I think maybe it's a horse or cow leg. Gross Jesse!"

I didn't have any type of rag with me, so I had to take it from her with my bare hands. It was probably the nastiest thing I have ever had to touch. It's a good thing that years ago I had worked in a nursing home changing bed pans and diapers, and cleaning the wheelchairs...it helped to prepare me for all the repulsive things Jesse brought home or rolled in.

I threw the leg into the bushes and yelled at her to stop when she went to retrieve it. Fine time to pretend you're a retriever Jesse. I turned to her as she walked back towards us and asked Kelly, "What in the world am I going to do with her? Look at her. Oh this is great." Jesse had exhibited the instinctual behavior of rolling and sliding in what I found out later, was a dead cow that had been decomposing since spring. She had taken one of its back legs to bring back with her as a prize—after covering her neck and shoulder with the remains.

"Good thing I live in Monte Carlo," Kelly called to me as she sauntered towards the parking lot.

"What? Monte Carlo? What are you talking about?" I was confused.

"You know, Monte Carlo, my car. I have a bar of soap in there; you can have it."

"Great, thanks…. Man! I sure don't want to do this. She is unbelievably disgusting. C'mere Jesse." I took the soap from Kelly, brought Jesse to the water and commenced to try to clean the decomposed remains of dead cow off of her thick white coat, while trying to persuade the contents of my stomach to stay where they belonged. It was hideous.

But at least she was white. This made it easier to see what I was doing whenever I had to clean off manure, or dead fish, or dead cow, or whatever else she found to use as dog perfume. I was very grateful for her white coat. I don't know how she did it, but she always managed to find something really gross and smelly to roll in and it didn't matter if we were in the country, in a park in the center of the city, at a friend's or by the lake.

Chapter 16

Ever since Jesse joined the ranks of water dogs of the lakes, our life at Percy Priest changed dramatically. Now we could go out in boats and I wouldn't be afraid that she'd drown if she accidentally fell in. She had always been perfectly capable —she had simply chosen to embarrass me, forcing me to be the mom of a non-swimming retriever. But now I knew she could swim with the best of them and I was proud.

My friend John had a sheepdog named Amos and an old wooden boat. We spent a good deal of time on the boat during the summer; water skiing and running around the lake visiting boats, while the dogs held their noses into the speeding wind while smelling the scents of the lake. Sometimes John's wife's brindle boxer named Cory was with us and they all loved to dive off the front of the boat and swim around in the cool water while we were anchored, but getting them back into the boat was a challenge at times. Their light water weight disappeared the moment they hit the surface.

We had a lot of fun at the lake and realized that there are some advantages to working at night. During the time when people with day jobs are working in the air-conditioned offices, we're running around water skiing and having fun in the great out doors. We might be getting skin cancer, but while we're working, they're sitting inside watching TV and ruining their eyes. There's always a trade-off.

So, because of my aversion to being sweaty—unless there was water around to jump into to relieve the heat—it seemed that I lived at the lake. But the lake was beautiful, the sun was hot, I loved to water-ski and when I was still working at night, why not? There were days when I'd go out to the lake to read, end up meeting really fun people and go water-skiing with them. I don't recommend this to anyone nowadays as there are simply too many wackos out there, but fifteen years or so ago, you could feel safe if you used good judgement. Sure, getting into a boat with strangers to be whisked off to go skiing. And how is that good judgement? Well maybe I was just lucky, or the Good Lord really felt sorry for me and my naiveté and kept an especially good eye on me, I don't know, but I do know that I never had anything bad happen to me. Besides, "I-just-might-bite-you-if-you-hurt-my-mom." Jesse was with me.

Actually, until we were on another trip to Kingsport to go visit my friends, I had no idea that Jesse ever would protect me because she seemed to be so indifferent to my presence most of the time. She was far more concerned with what treat Betty might have in the bowl on the floor in the kitchen, or finding a smelly thing to roll in, than to be concerned about her mom's safety.

It was late summer and we went to the back woods, and I do mean back—deep, deep in the hollers to an absolutely beautiful small farm. In the center of this incredibly peaceful farm, nestled in the soft hands of the Appalachian Mountains, was a sentimental old cabin. It was built in the late 1800's and had such character, that you almost expected to see Ma and Pa Kettle materialize right in front of your eyes. Hand-clapping foot-stomping yee-hawing fiddle music seemed to quietly drift from the centers of the logs that were the walls.

The cabin had great porches, both front and back, with wonderful serene views in all directions. My friends and some of their family members whom I had not previously met sat around on the front porch one evening, shooting the breeze, telling jokes and carrying on. They made me feel just like I was one of the family—we all had so much fun.

Down the hill in front of the cabin and around the bend in the grove of trees, was a small swimming hole. If you have ever been in the south in the late summer, you know that it continues to stay quite warm until late in the day, so swimming in the evening is a lovely experience—and this swimmin' hole was a'callin.

Dusk was dawning and some of us decided to go for a dip. As I was swimming in the refreshing coolness of the quiet pond, Jesse was exploring around the edges of the water. Their Uncle Bill had stayed up at the cabin, but was walking down through the trees, on his way to join us at the pond. Suddenly, Jesse jumped in and swam towards me, growling and holding her head very high in the water. She commenced to swim strong circles around me, never quite looking away from Uncle Bill and emitting a deep-throated growl. When she passed closely to me, I saw that her eyes had a piercing look that I had never seen before. I was shocked by her action. She had never displayed any protective behavior before, and although she had met this man—he shouldn't have been a threat—something told her to protect me. I was thrilled to discover that she had it in her to act like a normal devoted dog, but I thought she picked the wrong time to do this. Uncle Bill wasn't going to harm me and of course he didn't, but Jesse protected me and I'll never know why. I told Jesse she was a good girl for doing what she did, but she had met him so it was unnecessary. She calmed down eventually but stayed beside me, still looking around with a wary expression on her face. I was confused, but I trusted her and it was a wonderful feeling to know that my nonchalant dog might actually try to protect me if I was ever in danger. I was very proud and the great love I felt for her actually grew that day.

Since I knew that Jesse would protect me if I was in trouble, or at least would give the impression that she would, I felt safe on the boats. We had a terrific time meeting people, riding in the different boats and skiing up and down the channels of Percy Priest Lake. Jesse learned to be a good mast figure; standing with her paws on the bows of the boats, leaning into the wind and smelling all the fun and different smells that drifted across the water. All her experience of riding in the back of my truck gave her the ability to hold her position no matter where the boat was going and she never fell.

She loved riding in the back.

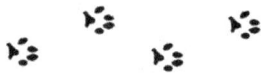

Chapter 17

She never fell out of a boat, but she still at times insisted on jumping out of the truck when I was going into a store. She never jumped out when it was moving; she thought that was something only dumb dogs do. Little did she know that it was almost just as stupid to leave the confines and safety of the truck to try to find me, which is what I think she was doing when she jumped. I even had my doubts about that however, when she would on occasion keep shopping after she found me. She really got to know where everything was at the Food Town in Old Hickory, where I bought the fish, but she never really had the chance to get to know the Kroger in Madison.

In her defense, it was a much bigger store and the one time she tried to shop there, they threw her out. It was on a Friday afternoon, after everyone and their brother had been paid, and everyone and their brother were in that particular Kroger, that particular day. I don't usually shop on Friday afternoons, but I was really in the mood for ice cream and I happened to be going by Kroger. So I parked the truck and got out to instruct Jesse very nicely.

"Jesse, I have to go and get just one thing OK?"

"So you want me to stay here?"

"Yes Jesse. Please. I won't be long."

"Why are there so many people here?"

"Because it's Friday and... oh never mind Jess, just do me a favor OK?"

"Sure Mom."

"Please. Stay...in...the...truck."

"But, why can't..."

"Jesse. If you don't mind, it's best for you to stay in the truck. I really don't want you jumping out. You're safe here."

"O-kaaay."

I went in and scurried towards the frozen foods section of the store and was looking at the flavors of ice cream, trying to decide between chocolate chip, and cookies and cream. As I was reaching for cookies and cream, I heard this announcement: "Attention shoppers. We have a big white dawg at the front of the store. Would the owner please come and get your dawg."

Jesse! Shoot. She jumped out of the truck again. And I had been so specific and polite with her in my request for her to stay.

I grabbed the ice cream and ran around the corner of the aisle, passing the two girls who were making pizzas on the front counter. As I was quickly sailing by, I heard one of them slowly drawl, "Musta, been, her, dawg."

I turned and briefly nodded as I glimpsed both of their heads calmly turning in unison towards me watching me run, while their hands kept slowly and methodically sprinkling cheese on the pizzas. They didn't miss a beat.

As I neared the check-out aisles, I felt the buzz of excitement and heard the comments.

"Look mama! Look at the dawg!"

"Hey, look, there's a big ol' dawg over there."

"What's a dawg doing in here?"

"Oh what a pretty dawg."

Yeah she's pretty all right, she's pretty in trouble. I saw her whipping around the lines of people—and don't think for a moment she was scared. Her tail was wagging so hard that her whole butt was shaking. I think she thought she was at a party. The store manager finally caught her (which was not an easy task), and as I caught up to him by snaking my way through the people, he said, "I'm sorry ma'me, but she can't be in here."

"I know and I'm really sorry, I'll take her. Sorry." I looked at him and grimaced.

"She really is a beautiful dawg," he whispered in my ear.

"Yeah thanks, but not right now, she's a bad dog," I retorted, as I led her out to the truck, put her in the cab, and left her shouting because I spoiled her party, while I went back for the ice cream that I had tossed on the end of the check out stand. It was a while before I shopped at that Kroger's again.

By now I had some more photography jobs and I worked on some photo shoots during the evening for The Nashville Network, so sometimes I took drives or went to the lake after work to unwind. I think I'm simply a night person by nature, which makes me think of another study. My theory, which has been richly substantiated over the years, is that generally speaking, if you're born in the morning, you're a morning dove, and if you're born at night, you're a night owl. If you're born during the afternoon or in the middle of the night, you swing either way and can adjust with ease to changing schedules. Just a theory.

I decided that night shopping was better, and for various reasons, some times I'd have Jesse with me when I stopped at the Food Town late at night. When she was first learning the layout of the store, I'd catch a glimpse of her strolling down the aisles and peering up at the shelves, so I'd run and catch her and put her back outside. Then she learned that if she stood on the mat, the door would stay open. She'd look longingly into the store, but stayed on the mat and took the time to greet the late night shoppers as they passed by and petted her on the head. It didn't do any good to put her back into the truck; either she'd jump back out, or if I put her in the cab, she'd wail so loudly that she was more annoying than listening to the buzzer that went off when she was standing on the mat. The guys liked Jesse and didn't really mind when she'd stand on the mat, holding the door open so she wouldn't miss anything. They simply learned to adjust to Jesse's visits.

"Hey Mike! Jesse's here, cut the buzzer." They'd turn off the buzzer, I'd shop for my few groceries, they'd turn it on again, and off we'd go till next time. Sometimes I'd have to remind them to turn the buzzer back on after we left. They were great guys.

You might think, wow, what an undisciplined dog. Well, she could be, but many times she would stay in the truck. It was random conduct. I asked a couple of vets over the years about that problem. I wondered if it could have had anything to do with the fact that she was an orphan and abandoned by her litter mates when she was so young. They both said yes, it very well could be. But since there wasn't any consistency to this behavior, it was hard to fix or to figure. I will say that she kept our time together quite interesting for me.

Her winter weather travel location.

Chapter 18

I think I made Jesse's life interesting for her too. Not necessarily setting out to entertain my dog, it's just how it happened to work out. "She traveled more than most people I know," was what my friend Janet always said about Jesse. She did see many parts of the lower forty-eight states, journeyed up to Alaska and all around Canada with me. We traveled some routes so frequently, that I probably could have given her the wheel if I had to.

My immediate family was in Illinois for the most part, so we became very familiar with the route from Nashville to Chicago, generally taking the Evansville, Indiana way instead of going through southern Illinois. One time Gina, Jesse and I went through Evansville on the way to visit her uncle in Lawrenceville. She curiously asked why their airport was called Evansville Regional Dress Airport and I quipped, maybe because it's on the outskirts of town. Sorry, but it was funny at the time. Evansville is nicknamed "The Stoplight" by the truckers, because there are more stoplights in that town than in a stoplight factory and if you don't hit the pattern just right, your travel time is all messed up. But it didn't bother me too much as I wasn't usually in a hurry. When you travel long distances with a dog, you tend to stop frequently to give them water, exercise, and time to pee.

Another time we went through The Stoplight, my brother Bob was with me. He had a female shepherd mix named Sasha who was another of Jesse's friends. Well, Sasha had gotten herself bloated with about 9 pups, and our sister wanted a female. So when the puppy was old enough to travel, it was time for a road trip.

The night we decided to go happened to be the start of a "Summer Nights" street fair event and we wanted to see it. So we planned to leave after work, pop by the fair and then drive through the night. We also figured it would be cooler for Jesse by traveling then.

It was the middle of the night by the time we were through Evansville, and now we all had bursting bladders. We wanted to get to the far side of town since we had hit the pattern just right and didn't want to break it. Jesse was riding in the back for the long journey on this beautiful summer's eve, while the pup was inside with us. As we drove into the parking lot of the gas station, I noticed a couple of guys standing by a pick up truck, watching us pick a parking spot. When we stopped and were getting out of the truck, one of the guys walked over to say hello and started petting Jesse. We all talked for a moment, and he seemed nice enough so Bob and the puppy walked away from the truck to relieve the youngster's bladder.

"This sure is a nice dog," he commented as he was slowly petting Jesse.

"Yeah, she's a pretty good girl," I smiled.

"She a lab?"

"No, she's half golden retriever, half white shepherd."

"That's a good combo. Smart dog I bet."

"Oh she's smart all right. Sometimes too smart for her own good."

"Does she hunt?"

"Jesse? Hunt?" I laughed loudly. "That's pretty funny. No, no, she doesn't hunt." Shaking my head with a chuckle.

"She'd make a great hunting dog," he seemed convinced.

"Not Jesse. She wouldn't bring anything back. She'd keep on running and keep it for herself, I know." I told him honestly.

"Well, she's a nice dog." He replied as he gave her a big pet then walked off to go inside.

Bob was still out with the pup, so I puttered around the truck, not wanting to leave it unattended.

I was getting Jesse out of the back, when the guy came over to me and quietly told me, "Don't leave your dog alone. My buddy wants to take her."

"What!?"

"Says she'd make a good hunting dog."

"Oh, get outa here. You're just kidding!" I laughed.

"Nope. Watch her." He was dead serious and suddenly I felt it.

"You're not kidding."

"No."

"Oh my gosh. Wow... I don't know what I'd do if she was gone." I paused and tried to let this news sink in as my heart started beating wildly. "Thank you so much for telling me!" I stood by my truck petting Jesse as I watched him walk back to his truck. I started shaking in disbelief. I was shocked that someone would actually steal a dog, just like that. Who would steal a dog?

I saw Bob and the pup returning and as they got closer to the truck I walked towards them with Jesse. When he passed me, he asked me what the guy wanted. I told him. He stopped.

He couldn't believe it either. Who would steal a dog? I was still in shock as I took my Jesse away to pee and was mulling over in my mind what had just happened.

That day at the lake when I was going to give her away was long, long ago and she was my best friend. I was immensely grateful to that man and we never let her out of our sight.

We made it to Sycamore that morning and delivered the puppy whom they named Dolly. Dolly grew into a beautiful dog and she and Jesse were friends for years. They even had a few fun adventures together before Dolly had to go and live on a farm outside of Sycamore. But we never forgot that trip when Jesse might have ended up having her photo on a milk carton.

Since I usually traveled through Indiana I was lucky enough on one trip to experience the folks that resided in the small and friendly place called Oaktown. It was in the winter and we were heading home for the holidays when I had truck trouble. Chevy Luv trucks were notorious for trouble with the fuel filters and we were near Oaktown when it happened. The truck started sputtering and hopping along the road; lurching forward then stalling, then gassing again to jump forward only to jerk backwards and stop before jumping ahead again. I had to put my arm out to hold Jesse, to keep her from hitting the dashboard, all while trying to shift and drive.

I pulled to the side of the snowy road and stopped the truck. A very sweet couple stopped to see if I needed help, which I did, and they told me to follow them. So we hopped and bounced behind them as they slowly led us to a service station in town that was just a block off the main road. It was during one of those nasty storms that come up in the Midwest, when the wind blows the snow and everything else sideways, so I was relieved when I was able to drive right into the garage to get the truck worked on.

While getting out of the truck, I told Jesse that she'd be fine in there, but the man came up to me and said that she'd be all right in the garage. So I let her out and she started to stretch her legs, cruising around in the work area.

I told the mechanic that the truck was acting like it wasn't getting enough gas, coughing and sputtering, and going like this...and I'm sure that auto mechanics get such a laugh out of the way most women describe their problems to them— making various noises and imitating an engine to the best of their ability. He said it was probably the fuel filter. Apparently they can get water in them, especially in this type of weather. He happened to have one, which I thought was lucky because this was not a particularly popular truck and we were in a small town.

It took about five minutes to change the filter and sure enough he poured water out of it, so that was the trouble. During this quick process, Jesse was still in the work area sniffing around, and only once did I have to tell her to stay in there with us. I asked the mechanic how much and he said five bucks. Wow! What a deal! Turning and heading through the doorway towards the counter to pay, I noticed some men sitting at a table in the corner playing checkers. As I walked into the small room I was immediately zapped into Floyd's barbershop

115

on the set of The Andy Griffith Show. At least it felt that way
to me. The four older gentlemen were simply relaxing and
enjoying each 's company. Men being men.

The room was definitely a male domain, yet it had a warm
and comfortable, and almost homey feeling to it. The calendars
on the wall had photos of cars and nature scenes—not of
scantily clad women like you see many times in garages, and I
think that led to the welcoming atmosphere. There was a thick
air of friendliness and fun that wafted throughout the small
room along with the scent of oil and grease.

The men looked up and grinned a friendly "Hi and Merry
Christmas," to me and I greeted them back with a big smile and
the same. I was relieved that it wasn't a serious mechanical
problem with my truck on this stormy day, and I shared the
Holiday Spirit.

Since I figured that this was the office part of the garage I
didn't want Jesse in there, so I turned towards her and said,
"Jesse, stop." She stopped. I snapped my fingers once. She sat.
I snapped again. She lay down. We had come a long way in the
discipline departments of her life and had sort of a secret
signal system. I turned back around to see the four men in the
corner peering at me, full of wonder. One man slowly drawled,
"That dog listens better than my wife."

We all chuckled and I said, "Yeah, well..." I didn't know
what to say without insulting his wife.

He continued very slowly, "Can I trade your dog for my
wife?"

That sent the men into a chorus of deep laughter—slap-
ping each on the back and laughing with their friend while
shifting their weight in their creaking chairs. I laughed and said,
"Well, Jesse's not much of a cook," assuming that his wife was,
as I assessed his rather large size.

"Neither is his wife!" retorted the bravest of the jokesters. That sent them into another round of booming laughter and I could still hear it consuming that cozy building as I gathered Jesse, said thank you to the mechanic and headed north in the snow storm.

They had just met.

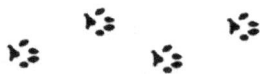

Chapter 19

On our way to Chicago, we always stopped in Champaign to visit with Janet, Mike and Raleigh. Raleigh was a beautiful golden retriever whose coloring was actually deep red, and he was three months older than Jesse. The first time Jesse met Raleigh, they were both two years old. It was love at first sniff. Theirs was a love that lasted over the years and miles of separation, never wavering in its strength. Even when they saw each in their later years, they still acted the same as they did when they first met.

It was amusing to watch how they had to be right next to each at all times, and if Raleigh got up to see something, Jesse had to go too. They followed each 's every move and were always touching each when they were lying down. They even shared rawhide toys, both chewing on the toy at the same time, in the fashion of "The Lady and the Tramp" spaghetti scene.

I have two pages of photos showing their first week together because we couldn't believe how they were acting. If dogs can be soul mates, Jesse and Raleigh certainly were. They knew each for almost thirteen years, and Jesse was the only dog whom Raleigh allowed into his territory without an argument. I have many photos documenting this long and distant love affair, showing how the two dogs aged. They were always sitting or lying together whenever we visited, no matter how old they were, or how long it had been since they'd seen each .

When they were young, they had great fun playing in the large back yard that sloped towards the ravine, making up games when they could. One winter when Jesse was staying there, (while I headed to Chicago in the times before I could bring her with me), they made their very own skating rink. Janet and Mike were gone for the day and when they returned home, they found that the whole yard was one big ice flow. The dogs were sliding downhill to the ravine, stopping at the fence, only to go running back up the side to the top and go slip sliding down. Janet and Mike watched them do this again and again, wondering how in the world they turned the faucet on to create this frozen flood, and why they would do this to begin with. None of us ever figured out that "Day at the Ice Rink" for those two smart dogs.

They say dogs don't remember places where they have been, or recognize landmarks, right? Wrong. When Raleigh lived on Dogwood and we'd turn the corner, Jesse would get all excited and start crying with happiness because she knew that she was going to see Raleigh. On Springfield Avenue, as we came near to the big white house, she'd start wagging her tail and dancing around the truck. Later when Raleigh moved to Washington Street, it took one, only one time, for her to know where we were going. Once I did an experiment. I didn't even mention Raleigh's name and she was still so excited when we turned the corner by his street. I don't believe everything the experts say, because I have experienced a dog's memory first hand many times and if you have a dog, you probably have too. Jesse certainly remembered Raleigh her entire life.

Another dog Jesse remembered was Mindy. Jesse visited with Mindy for only two holidays, and even though Mindy was quite old when they met, they were instantly friends. "Respecting your elders" *was* in her program. She knew Mindy was old and moved very gingerly around her. But they didn't play together. They just sat around like old dogs. It was interesting to watch and I wondered about that dog sense that just knows certain things. They know when you're leaving for a trip and they aren't joining you, they know when you're hurting emotionally or physically, and they know when something's not quite right in your house before a fire or flood. They know a million things and we can't figure out how, but they know. And, they know when they've lost a friend.

The first time we went home after Mindy died, we walked in the front door and immediately, Jesse started whining and running into the kitchen, into the living room, into the dining room, up and down the stairs and all over the house. She was looking for Mindy. I quickly realized this and sat on the floor hugging and petting Jesse, trying to console her and be comforted by her presence, as I was also crying for the wonderful old dog whom I had known for eighteen years. Even Jesse's usually bright eyes had a certain dullness to them, and it took a while for her to settle herself. Her sadness was obvious as she moped around for the rest of the day, softly crying.

Yes, dogs know. They know when a dog is old, when a dog is young, and when a child is sticking their fingers in your nose, don't bite them. At least Jesse knew this. My sister has four children and Jesse was there for all of her children's childhoods. Our visits were sporadic, but we somehow managed to always catch at least one of the kids at the age of two or three, when their tiny child fingers fit perfectly inside the nostrils of a big dog.

Jesse would usually hang out with me during the day, unless people were around; she loved to sit with visitors. But she did sleep with me every night, either on the floor next to my bed in the summer or in the bed with me during the winter. And she didn't sleep at the bottom curled up like the classic photos. Oh no, Jesse put her head on the pillow, slept on her side, on her side of the bed and faced the outside edge. We'd usually be back to back but it always cracked me up to roll over and see her snoozing there like a person—with a furry white head. But if she started out on my side, I'd have to move her over. She'd softly and quietly growl at me, but not move a muscle to help...stubborn shepherd.

At my sister's, I usually slept on the hide-a-bed in the living room, and there were many mornings when I awoke to the quiet laughter of young children by the side of the bed. I would roll over to look down at my nieces or nephew and see them putting their fingers inside Jesse's nostrils, or lifting her ears and peering inside, giggling at what they saw. I guess they were fascinated at the small black holes of her nose that accommodated their fingers so snugly and comfortably, and the patterns and caverns that the furry flaps of her ears revealed when they were lifted up. The kids had their own soft and friendly action book of things to do; things to lift, things to press, and things that made them laugh. Amazingly, she never got mad at them for doing this. When she'd had enough, she simply moved to a spot underneath the end table where they couldn't get to her. Every one of them experienced the live book of Jesse and she never ever growled at any of them. She knew better.

Typical Irish Scene

Chapter 20

I knew better, but it seemed I couldn't help my feelings or my actions. That Sunday, when we left Greenane, I was in a fog of emotions. Something had happened to me the night before concerning this Irish fisherman, and I was in another world. I even hit a curb for the first time in the history of my -side-of-the-road driving. That night, I called Sean to get a number where I could try to reach Danny. Sean gave me two numbers and I tried and tried to get through, but was completely frustrated by the system and difficulty of calling the Republic of Ireland from Northern Ireland using phone cards. I was especially frustrated because I couldn't remember exactly what I had dialed to get through to Sean in the first place. But I was determined and finally reached one of the pubs, but Danny had left. I told Patrick, the republican (pub owner) that I would try again on Monday evening around eight; "Aye that's fine, you do that."

For the next two evenings while the girls and I were still traveling around together, I tried to reach Danny. Patrick was helpful in my quest by calling Danny's house a few times, and he even sent his son to the pier to see if Danny's boat was there, but we still couldn't find him. Something inside me, made me have to talk to him again, no matter what the outcome. I couldn't understand what was going on, but there was something about him. I just didn't know what. I wasn't acting like myself; calling and calling for some man whom I had just met and had been with for only about ten hours. But, I wasn't eating or sleeping either.

I didn't reach him.

The girls were leaving early on Wednesday morning and as B was packing, she was speaking words of wisdom to me.

"Don't drive all the way up there without talking to him first. Patti, that wouldn't be smart." She told me.

"Oh I would never do that." I replied honestly.

"And don't you dare take your mom up there. If I was her and you did that, I would be furious with you. Going up to see some guy you just met; not a good idea." She warned me.

"Oh, I know B, but I just really want to see him again or at least talk to him." I sadly replied as I knew the reality of the situation.

"Patti, what if you did see him again, then what? Do you want to try to have a long distance relationship and be miserable when you're apart, like Pete and Eve?" (My old housemate who fell in love with a French girl who lives in Ireland, where, by the way, I am sitting in their house awaiting Christmas in Killarney.)

"Don't get me wrong, if you got in touch with him and went up there and had a great time, there's nothing wrong with that, but then what? Look at the emotional wreck you are now and it would only get worse. Do you want a relationship where you see that person a couple of times a year? Would you move to Ireland if things were to develop into something? What about your horse, what would you do? You have to think about these things." She spoke to me with the concern of a wonderful friend.

"Yeah, I know I know, you're right. I just don't understand why I'm feeling like this, and don't worry, I won't bring Mum up there, I won't."

I took the girls to the airport on Wednesday morning and now I was on my own until Saturday when I had to pick up my mom in Dublin. I drove towards the Wicklow Mountains that I had loved so much the last time I was in Ireland, and it took me far longer than planned because I went through the heart of Dublin by mistake. Reaching the Wicklows in the late afternoon, I was cruising around the peaceful countryside, stopping to pet horses and trying not to think about Danny. But I couldn't stop thinking about him and at one point I had an American moment in a bad way. I drove on the wrong side of the road, nearly having a head-on collision. I decided that I'd better stop driving or I'd kill myself or worse, hurt someone else. I took out the map and decided to head to Roundwood, which unbeknownst to me at the time, is the highest village in Ireland. That was fitting, seeing as I came from one of the highest communities in the Rocky Mountains of Colorado.

Slowly driving through town, I discovered a field that contained a number of farm trucks and trailers. I was in the right spot. It was the weekly sheep sale and annual ram show, so there were farmers from the whole district. I procured a room, headed to the pub and settled into a night of Guinness, award presentations, farmer stories, and loads of laughs. But I never gave up trying to reach Danny and every so often, I'd go out to the outdoor phone booth and try again. I spoke to his brother Thomas many times and at one point, his mother said for him to give me Danny's mobile number, which I tried to no avail. I was surprised that they were as helpful and tolerant as they were, taking it as a good sign.

As I was ready to call it a night, I was intercepted by the guy who was at the pub, by the phone booth, that I had bopped into to get a pen to write Danny's number down, and he and his friend asked if I wanted to come up for a nightcap. Oh sure, what the heck. They were staying down the hall from me, so I went in, but my nightcap was water... I'd had enough. They were interesting young men who were counselors at the local camp for problem boys, and we talked about their job, living in the Wicklow Mountains and life in Colorado. I inadvertently told them the fact that I was an emotional mess over a man whom I had just briefly met. Instead of berating me on my female foolishness, they thought it was wonderful. I told them I really wanted to see this man again and was fighting against rational thinking. They assured me I wasn't crazy, just rather romantic and that I should go back up to see him. They actually encouraged me to go.

Romantic or crazy, I'm not sure. But this I do know. When I went driving around the area the next day, trying to dispel Danny from my mind by enjoying the beauty of the mountains and the splendor of the views, it wasn't working. My mind was fighting my heart and my heart was fighting my mind. I wanted to go and try to see him, but it didn't make any sense to drive halfway across a country to try to see a man whom I barely knew, but who seemed to have a hold on my heart.

Three years ago in Colorado, I was intrigued by a Swiss skier whom I met one evening at a local saloon where the whole Swiss Olympic Ski team was whooping it up. I had been through his hometown merely two weeks earlier and we had fun dancing and spent a great time in conversation. I have occasionally thought about him and wondered about his interesting life and wished that I could have learned more about him, but I never saw him again. I thought of him this day and in one instant my mind was made up. I wasn't going to pass up the slim chance that I might see Danny again and end up wondering what would have happened. I had to try. I was going back to Greenane. I called Sean and left a message for him to save me a room; I was coming back. The fight was over. My heart won.

Jesse and Raleigh...playing.

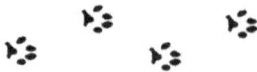

Chapter 21

OK, you people with the perfect dogs might want to skip this part as I'm sure this would never happen with your dog. It has to do with the fact that every now and then, dogs have arguments with each and they tend to use their teeth; not just giving lip service.

Jesse was not a fighter by nature, so she didn't have too many fights. Maybe she thought fighting was just too dog-like, I don't know. But I thought it was interesting, that the only fights she did have were with dogs of the Husky breed. I honestly didn't understand why that was. But after the fight she had with a Husky on the trail one day, I learned to turn and go the way whenever we would see one. Sure added an element of suspense to our walks. "There's a Husky. Quick, Jesse! Let's go this way!" as I'd whisk her away to avoid a confrontation. Maybe it was because of a Husky she met when she was young who was not very nice to her. This dog's name was Anya and she belonged to some friends of Janet and Mike's. Remember? Raleigh's parents.

On those occasions when I had to leave Jesse with Janet, Mike and Raleigh to go to Park Ridge for Christmas, Jesse would sometimes see Anya. They argued at first sight. Anya was younger, which made it unlikely that Jesse would fight with her because she liked younger dogs, but unfortunately, they fought. Jealousy over Raleigh would be my guess, because he was quite the handsome fellow.

Janet told me about one incident that happened when she and Mike were babysitting Jesse and Anya. One night, they discovered all three dogs in the bed with them—very tight squeeze or really big bed, I'm not sure. Anya was on one side, Jesse on the and Raleigh was in the middle. Anya was glaring and growling at Jesse, while Raleigh was snoring away, oblivious to everything. The estrogen tension was mounting, but before the girls had a chance to see who would be sharing rawhide with Raleigh, Janet kicked all three dogs off the bed and separated Jesse and Anya. Poor Raleigh got the short end of that stick, but bloodshed was avoided.

Sticks and balls. Oh yeah... Remember, Jesse wasn't really a retriever, so she never had that retriever obsession with sticks and balls. I was glad, because many of Jesse's friends were true retrievers and there were enough arguments over sticks, without Jesse getting in on the action. While the dogs would be back on the trail duking it out, Jesse would be off wandering around with her tail wiggling in the air, looking like a big question mark. It was her happy go lucky mode, but maybe it was also her way of asking, "What's the big deal with the sticks anyway? I don't get it."

If you are going to have a dog that is prone to fighting, I'd highly recommend getting one with a good strong tail. It comes in handy if you're going to break up the brawl. Not that trying to get in the middle of gnashing teeth and whirling dog bodies is the safest thing to do, but tails are helpful.

One time Jesse and I were visiting my friend John, when Amos and Corey were not seeing eye to eye over the lovely neighbor who was in heat. We were all hanging out in the yard casually talking, enjoying the cool evening air, when suddenly the male dogs were at each 's throats. I watched, feeling helpless —as the blurred mass of brown and black, and white and gray fur was whipping frantically around in the yard, while the angry thunder of growling dogs filled the air. I wasn't sure what I should do to try to stop this massive quarrel. John waded into the snarling tangle of canines yelling, "Amos! Corey! Cut it out! Corey! Amos! Patti! Don't stand there, help me!"

"But they don't have tails, John! They don't have tails!" I shouted back to him. I was jumping up and down and dancing nervously around the mass, trying to step forward to help, but backing away when the dogs came too close to my legs. I didn't want to get bitten, and since there wasn't anything to grab on to, I wasn't getting involved—no way. I simply couldn't help him with his dogs.

John was finally able to separate the boys, but during the ruckus, Amos nailed him squarely in the arm. Chomp! I felt bad for John and tried to explain my aversion to getting bitten, as we went into the house to doctor his arm. I wasn't going to get in the middle of a dogfight when I couldn't pull them apart from the back. Tails don't bite. They didn't have tails. You don't get help. I'm sorry.

One of my Irish friends, Liam, told me a tale about his mom's wirehaired terrier named Teddy. His mom ran a boarding house in their small town and had to go to the store everyday to replenish the supplies for the twenty or so guests who would stay with them.

He said, "Every single time, she would start her errand by sitting Teddy at the door. She would lean down, wag her finger at him, look him straight in the eye and tell him, 'Sure Teddy. You can go with me to the store today, only if you promise not to be fightin'.'

'Aye, promise. No fightin' today,' said he, looking up at her with mournful brown eyes. So off to the store they'd go, walking happily down the street enjoying the fresh air. But soon after arriving at the store, where dogs and people alike were out visiting, sure enough Teddy would see someone with whom he had unfinished business and start a fight."

Liam couldn't remember exactly what breed of large dog Teddy's pal was, but said, "This, not-so-wee dog would be assisting Teddy with his argument. Sure when Teddy saw that his friend had everything under control, aye, he'd trot off and be gone. He just pretended that nothing had happened a 'tall. Oh I tell ya that Teddy, he was a sly dog."

Due to the fact that I prefer the "tail method" of breaking up dog fights, I have been bitten only once... by Jesse. It was a beautiful, balmy spring day and we were up at Betty and

Claude's just relaxing in the back yard, sitting in lawn chairs shooting the breeze, and watching the world go by—as is the pleasant and popular pastime in the South. Well, she had an itch on her neck, and when she scratched it, her toenail got stuck in the chain. The howl that she let out woke up the dead, and at least half of Hopewell. I jumped over to her even though I knew better than to try to help an injured, un-muzzled dog. As I was releasing her toenail, she bit me. This happened in a split second and I quickly stepped away from her to assess the damage. Luckily she got the boney part of my wrist, so her tooth didn't penetrate. I could tell that she felt bad, and we both knew that I should have reacted differently, but it just happened too fast. If you'd heard a howl like the one she screamed that day, you'd probably do the same. So that was my one and only dog bite and I would really like to keep it that way.

Ridin' around with her buddy Sackett.

Chapter 22

"Hi there Claude. Mmmm, something smells good. Whatcha cookin?" I said one day when we went for a visit. "What's in here?" I asked as I lifted the lid from the pot that was bubbling away on the old white stove, and leaned over to enjoy the wonderful aroma.

"Blackie. Makin' soup." He stated nonchalantly.

"Eeuuww!" I dropped the lid as if it had burned my fingers. Luckily it landed back onto the pot that contained the beautiful black banty rooster whom I had seen pecking for seeds the day before.

OK now, this is a problem for me. I have always wanted to get back to the farm, but there is no way I can eat something that I had just seen cruising around the yard the day before, especially if it had a name. I like seeing animals running around and having fun without the threat of being in a pot, so I knew that I would have no part of this fowl soup that I had to admit smelled quite appealing.

Most of the aromas that floated out of that kitchen invited the taste buds to enjoy a splendid meal, and I was going to miss them dearly.

I had been living in Tennessee for over six years and was in need of a change. While out on the lake one day, John and I drove from the cliffs to the cove, not talking over the engine noise, and when he stopped the boat I informed him, "John, I'm moving to Colorado at the end of next summer."

"Patti, you've been talking about moving to Colorado for years." He dismissed my statement with ease.

"I know, I've been saying that I'll move there eventually. But now I think it's time to move." I defended myself.

"Yeah sure, you're just going to pick up and move."

"Yup. I did when I came here, but I don't want to live here anymore. I want to go and live in Colorado." I told him confidently.

"Well we'll see," he laughed.

I spent the next year preparing for the move. I resumed working in the restaurant industry to facilitate getting a job when I landed in Denver. I thought that it would be hard to get work immediately as a freelance photographer, and I didn't want to be rusty with my waitress skills when applying for work. I continued with some of my photography clients and knew that I'd miss them when I left. My favorite was working for TNN, the country music cable station. I'd miss the people who worked there and the friendly country music stars that graced the TV screen, but it was time to move on.

I was thinking that Jesse would probably like to get to a cooler climate too. She seemed to pant the long summer days away when we were not at the lake, and a few years earlier, her mange had reappeared. This was much to the surprise of her vet, who had seen any mange resurface only one time in the sixteen years he had been practicing. But I treated her quickly, and now her coat had developed into a soft, thick and furry white blanket around her bones, for which I was grateful, but she seemed to be more and more uncomfortable in the heat.

But she did get heat relief when we were in the country, with the soft breezes and open spaces to explore, or the cool woods away from her doghouse. I had met a guy named Jay who lived outside of Mt. Juliet, and Jesse and I spent a lot of time at his house. She made friends with Sackett, a beautiful big boxer who belonged to his brother who lived next door. Jesse and Sackett would ride in my truck together, each on their own side and watch the world go speeding by. Sackett loved to catch the wind in his mouth. It opened up like a large mouth bass with huge teeth and I'm sure the people who saw this thought he was ferocious, but he really was a softy. Jesse enjoyed their casual friendship and looked forward to our frequent trips out to the country.

It was at Jay's house where she resumed her screen-eating behavior, and I just couldn't figure out why. Sometimes, she ate her way in and sometimes she ate her way out. I'd leave her outside and we would return to find her inside, with the living room screen torn in shreds. Sometimes Sackett was with her, sometimes not. So then I'd leave her in and return to find her outside running around, with the living room screen torn again. I didn't know if she sensed that we were in for a huge change in our lives, or what, but that was a puzzle I never solved. I just invested in a screen tool to fix the screens, and I sure used that tool a lot. She ate her way in at John's house, out at Wendy's place and ripped the whole patio screen at my pal Bobbie's house one evening. Neither rhyme nor reason existed for this expensive behavior, and although I had never planned on putting "Professional Screener" on a resume, I certainly could have.

At the beginning of that summer when I was to move, Joyce informed me that she was moving to Delaware to continue working at DuPont and I had to move right away because she was selling the house. Again I was in an unfortunate spot because I planned to move to Denver in August. Where was I going to live for a couple of months? Jay suggested that I live in his three-bedroom house, seeing as I was there so much anyway. So Jesse and I spent our last days of living in Tennessee out in the country, and we loved it.

I picked August eighth as my day to move, and when it came around, Jay followed me 'n Jess, as I drove my loaded truck that pulled a jam-packed U-Haul trailer to meet my old roommate Gloria. She had decided earlier that she wanted to live in Colorado too. So we met at the intersection of Old Hickory Boulevard and interstate 40, I said bye to Jay—I would keep in touch—and we started on the long drive to Colorado.

Chapter 23

The long drive from Roundwood in the Wicklow Mountains in the middle of Ireland, to Greenane, in the northern part of Ireland took me about seven hours of fast Irish driving. Since there are very few four-lane roads in Ireland, they have a system of driving that I have not found elsewhere in all of my travels to date.

When you're passing a car, you put your right turn signal on and leave it on as you're driving in the oncoming traffic's lane. This way, those cars that are speeding towards you move over onto their left shoulder in order to give you the space needed to drive in their lane, therefore passing the car in your lane. A matter of sharing the highway at its best. Usually, the car that you're passing moves over to your left shoulder, enabling you to pass. When they do this, you give them a flash of your emergency blinkers in a gesture of thanks.

Going through the small towns can really slow you down though, because the Irish have a tendency to park where they feel like it whether there's room or not. It must be a main reason why all the cars are relatively small—they can get around in the tight squeezes created by their methods of madness.

Actually, size has to do with taxes, but it certainly made for interesting motoring around the place. You have to be ready for anything that pops up around the bend and be on the lookout for cars in your lane at anytime. Doing all this, while remembering that technically, left is right, and right is left—if you're from a right-side-of-the-road-driving country.

So, stopping a few times to try to reach Danny on his mobile phone, to warn him I was on my way, I arrived at the B & B around seven thirty in the evening. This was after trying to reach Danny at home, when I stopped about three kilometers away. Again no luck, but I told his brother to let him know that I was in town. His brother knew I had been in the Wicklows that morning and was surprised that I was headed back to Greenane. It's like driving from Iowa to California relatively speaking. Nuts, I know.

Sean was on his way home with his friend Tim from Toronto, whom he had picked up at the airport. After they arrived, we visited briefly and then headed to the pubs to try to find Danny. Sean scouted, but we never found him, so we headed into O'Malley's for a pint. Danny's friend Ryan was sitting at the corner of the bar and when he saw me, he smiled, chuckled and said, "Aye Patti, I never expected to see you here again."

"Well I never expected to see me here again either, but I had to see Danny, I just don't know..." I stopped, looking down at the bar in my slight embarrassment.

"Well he won't be in," Ryan looked me squarely in the eye when I raised my head to look at him.

"He won't?" I asked.

"No. Certain. I was just down to the pier and know he's out on the boat tonight." He looked at me with a very serious expression.

"Certain?"

"Certain."

"Well, I guess I'll just have to try to see him tomorrow then, won't I?" I felt a mixture of disappointment and relief. Now I could visit with Sean and Tim and not be nervously watching for Danny. Even though I drove all this way to see him, I felt uneasy about having done such an irrational act, despite the fact that I knew in my heart...I had to do it. So I went to join Sean at the corner of the bar.

We sat and talked for half an hour about Canada (we had all lived in or near Toronto at some time), and I happened to be looking towards the door, when in walked one of the fishermen I recognized, and right behind him was who? Danny. I couldn't believe my eyes! My heart pounded its way out of my chest and I started shaking. I even had to steady myself by holding on to the edge of the bar. I had no idea that seeing him would have such an incredibly strong effect on me. How can that happen? I was shocked to say the least. I grabbed Sean's arm. "He's here!" I whispered loudly.

"Right then. I'll be leaving ya to yerself." Sean said as he started to turn away.

I put a vise grip on his forearm, "Sean! Don't leave me." I panicked.

"Oh for fect's sake, ya came all the way up here to see 'im, and he's here. Now go."

"I will. Give me a minute." I had to change gears in my head, breathe and calm down. I felt like an infatuated young girl. Maybe because I hadn't felt those emotions in so many years, I was confused as to how they had so easily seized my heart and held it in their powerful grasp. But they had. I went to the bathroom to compose myself and when I came out, I thought he was gone. But then I saw that he was sitting at a table, and I was so very nervous, when I went over to talk him.

"Hi." I paused, drinking in his handsome face. Then I sheepishly said, "I had to see if you're as cute as I thought you were, or if it was the Guinness." Yup, I really said that. It just popped out of my mouth. It was what I was thinking. My censoring ability had completely abandoned me.

He looked down and smiled, shaking his head. Then he looked up at me, smiled and said, "It was the Guinness."

The first moments were a bit awkward, as would be expected, and then he offered me a seat. I sat down and conversation started slowly, but we talked ourselves into a state of comfort and into the night. I was outwardly relaxed with him, but my heart had a hard time calming down. I thought when I had left him the day, I would never see him again and yet now, I was once again sitting next to him, watching him smile and listening to him tell stories about his life. I was happy and very relieved. I had no idea what his reaction would be to my showing up, especially without warning. It must have been fine, because there was laughter and good conversation all around. At one point, I told him that I didn't expect to see him that night. He said something on the boat broke, so they had to come in. Fate.

We eventually left the pub and walked along the dark road to the B&B, laughing and talking as we traveled together. When we arrived, I showed him the photos of my house, my horse and the mountains of Colorado. He was surprised that I thought Greenane was a great place, coming from the beauty of the mountains. I think that's a universal feeling—along the "greener grass on the side", line of thinking. No matter how spectacular it is where you live, after time, most people end up taking their area for granted. Sometimes it takes leaving them, to be reminded of just how beautiful your home surroundings really are.

We spent the late night talking, laughing and just being with each and when he was leaving, he invited me to come and see his boat the next afternoon. After a restless sleep, I got up and visited with Sean and Tim through the morning and into the lunch hour. When I left, I mentioned that I didn't have a key, and for them to please leave a way for me to get back into the B&B. "Aye, will do."

I drove to the pier to see how Danny made his living. He fished for oysters and salmon in seasons, but for now he was on the mussel boat. It was pretty intriguing to see the holding tank that could accommodate one hundred tons of mussels and I enjoyed watching the men work around the vessel. I didn't actually get on the boat. "'Tis bad luck to have a woman on the boat, aye, it is."

Ah yes, the Irish have their share of superstitions.

Danny agreed to meet me that night around seven and I returned to the B&B for a short nap. When I arrived, it was locked. I immediately knew that Sean had done this on purpose and I knew just where to look for the jokester. I found him and Tim at the pub.

"You locked me out on purpose!" I accused him, as I walked through the doorway of the nearly empty pub.

"Oh for feck's sake, of course I did. What, do ya think I'm stupid?" He laughed, as he ordered me a pint of Guinness.

So Sean, Tim, and I "had good craic" there, and next at O'Malley's until around five o'clock when I had to go and try to get that wee nap in. As I turned to leave, the door opened and in walked Danny. I was surprised, excited, exhausted and elated all at the same time. He was a bit surprised to see me too, but I joined him and we sat at the pub for hours—talking and laughing and carrying on. One patron shouted to me after she had been there for a few pints: "Aye Patti, I don't know what you've done to our Danny, but I've never seen him clean shaven on a Friday night in all me life!"

Danny was embarrassed too, but he had a good sense of humor. When we left the pub, he gave me a lift back to the B&B. Sean was in the kitchen cooking when Danny and I came in, so they chatted for a while; remembering the old days when Danny was growing up and worked for different people. Sean proceeded to inform me that Danny indeed had mowed the grass at the B&B when he was a wee boy. "Aye. Danny was a good boy."

Danny and I sat around the B&B for a while and then ended up driving around in the rain, going to the ends of the roads, looking down at the sea and listening to the waves as they crashed against the rocks. We drove around the area, seeing the lights and sights and talking about growing up in Greenane. I was getting to know Danny better, I really enjoying being with him and I realized that my feelings for him were getting even stronger. I didn't know what it was about him, but he had a strong hold on my heart. I can guess it was the whole "American-on-vacation-in-a-magical-place-like-Ireland" thing, but I suspect that it was more than a superficial assessment of the situation. He was special, I knew it, and I wanted to spend more time with him. This was unfortunate. I was leaving to go and pick up my mom in Dublin in the morning—without plans to return to the area and with strict instructions not to.

"I want to come and see you again," I told him, as he was leaving.

"When?" he asked, surprise in his voice.

"In two weeks. I'll change my plane ticket." I replied hopefully.

"Two weeks? No, that would be too dodgy, I'll be fishin'. You're talking shite anyway."

He never believed me, when I told him things that I thought, or felt about him. He was shocked that I drove all the way up to Greenane just to see him in the first place.

"Really. I would change my ticket." I looked up at his smiling face.

We exchanged words, smiles, kisses and hugs, then slowly and reluctantly drifted apart.

"It's a once in a lifetime thing Patti, a once in a lifetime thing," he said, as he shyly shrugged his shoulders, grinning at me. "I really have to go."

The expression he wore as he left, his handsome face, and his beautiful smile is etched into my memory forever.

As I watched him go away, I honestly thought that this time, I would never see him again. I stood at the bay window and watched him drive past the house, feeling completely numb inside.

Our first Sunday in Denver, we went up to Echo Lake.

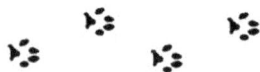

Chapter 24

I was sick inside when I discovered that I lost my wallet the day I drove up to St. Louis. (This is an important tangent by the way.) It was when the Tennessee Volunteers won the Sugar Bowl. I worked for a company that screened hats and t-shirts, and we ran out of the orange and white hats. I was asked to buzz up to St. Louis for some more hats. Impromptu 600 mile round trip road trip? Sure, no problem. The problem was that I lost my wallet at some time during the trip. I canceled credit cards and had to borrow twenty bucks from a lady at the hat company so I had money to get home. And, I didn't have my license, so I made sure I was the picture of a perfect driver.

But I was so very lucky, because I returned home to find that the group of guys I had seen goofing around by the Arch, had picked up my wallet that I left at the phone booth by the Arch. They called and left a message, but I had to wait until the next day to call them back because it was so late when I arrived home. I told them to keep any money inside and they happily agreed to mail my wallet back to me. We kept in contact for almost two years and when Jesse, Gloria and I were moving to Colorado, we stopped to meet them in Kansas City; where they lived. Really great guys who let us stay at their house (instead of camping out), and that hot shower sure was wonderful after a long day of traveling. They were both named Steve, which I thought was funny because they were roommates. So Steve, Steve, Gloria and I went to a softball game, out for pizza and had a very entertaining evening.

Steve had a dog named King who was part chow, part malamute, part shepherd and all giant. He towered over Jesse at the shoulder and was one of the two dogs in Jesse's life whom she feared. In the years that followed—when Jesse and I went back to Tennessee from Colorado—we'd go and see Steve 'n King. When we'd arrive, she absolutely would not get out of the truck until Steve put King in the back yard, and then, and only then, she'd come out very slowly—cautiously watching all around her for King the whole time. It was good to see the Queen Bee humbled for once, but I always made sure that she was comfortable while we were at Steve's. Humbled is one thing, scared is another.

When we eventually arrived in Denver, I called the Johnsons. They were friends of my Johnson friends, whom I knew from my church in Nashville. They had been in confirmation class together in Chicago long ago, and the Colorado Johnsons were expecting our call. They lived just ten minutes from where we happened to stop, and we were very glad to meet Pam and her dad Wes and we followed them to their house in Arvada. I was hoping that they would know where I could park my truck and trailer, while Gloria, Jesse and I camped. We'd try to find a place to live, meanwhile camping in the nearby foothills. Well, they wouldn't hear of it. They were gracious enough to let us stay at their house. They fed us and entertained us for over a week. Wes' wife Lucille even took us around one day looking for a place to live. They went way beyond any hospitality guideline possible and to this day I try to see them whenever I can—when I go to Denver from the mountains.

We found a place that we liked in the Sloan Lake area of west Denver. We called the landlords and I told the man that I had a dog. He said we could talk about it, just come over and see the place. We headed over to the cute little house that sat back from the street in a quiet neighborhood and went to the front door and knocked. A woman answered and told us her name was Sal. We said hello and introduced ourselves. She saw Jesse and immediately said that her husband Tony must have misunderstood me. They would not allow a dog of Jesse's size to live there. They'd had too many bad experiences with big dogs in the past. Bummer.

"Well, since we're new in town, could we see the place anyway so we can compare and see what the rentals are like in the area?" I asked them as they stood there looking at us.

"I suppose so, sure." Sal answered. "Where are you moving from?" she asked us, as we started to walk to the small back yard to put Jesse inside the fence, then we turned and walked in through the back door.

"We arrived from Nashville, Tennessee a few days ago." I told her, glad that she was friendly to us, despite my large dog.

"Nashville? Do you like country music?" Tony asked.

"You have to, if you live there," Gloria drawled back, smiling.

We went inside the house and I told Jesse to stay there and wait for us. We'd be right back. Sal, Tony, Gloria and I walked around this great house that would have been perfect for us. We talked about the area and had a friendly and pleasant conversation. We all got along very well and they commented that they were really sorry about the dog situation. They had a dog and loved dogs, but hoped we understood. I said I did, but that it's unfortunate for dog owners like me who take care of people's places. I added that Jesse was a five-year-old dog who was a good girl.

"Would it be possible for us to live here if we kept Jesse outside in the yard and she could stay in the back porch?" I asked, hoping that they might think about this option.

"We just really don't want a big dog here, I hope you..." Sal was saying to me, when Tony interrupted, "Sal, look."

We were standing in the dining room on the chocolate brown carpet, when Jesse came tiptoeing very, very, slowly into the kitchen, warily peering through the doorway. I realized she was looking for me, because when she saw me, her face was flooded with relief. When I saw her, I commanded, "Jesse, stop." I snapped my fingers at her. She stopped and sat down before setting a paw on the carpet. Relaxed, now that she found me, she just sat there watching us.

"Oh, she was looking for her mom," Sal softly smiled and crooned. She had observed Jesse's expression and mannerisms and said, "Tony, did you see how she tiptoed? She was so cute."

"Yeah, and she sure listens well, doesn't she Sal?" Tony looked at Jesse thoughtfully.

"Yes, she does, when she knows she better." I said honestly. "I don't want her stepping on that carpet with her white fur."

In the silent moments that followed, Sal and Tony changed their minds about the dog that Wes had nicknamed the White

152

Ghost. (He called her that because of the way she quietly snuck around their house, looking for their cat to play with.) Jesse had won them over with her tiptoe style and her semi-tuned listening skills. I was happy she chose that day to exhibit some of the training she had received in the past. I have to say "some", because she didn't stay and wait as I had told her to, but it didn't seem to matter. I think she knew what was going on and decided to be semi-well behaved, extra charming and cute. Well, it worked and we moved in by the end of the week. Yee haw! We were living in Denver.

Sal and Tony agreed that Jesse was a good dog and she could live with us inside the house. I was happy about that and thought we had really great landlords, which we did. So while Gloria and I went job searching, Jesse lounged around all areas of the house. We both landed jobs at this incredibly posh brand new country club, in the very small banquet department —if you could call it that—it was basically four people. We were very part-time to start with, so I found another job at a restaurant named Chad's, on the west side of Lakewood, which had an atmosphere very similar to the TV show "Cheers".

A couple of weeks later, I came home after my Monday day shift and was excited because the Johnson boys were coming over to watch the Broncos on Monday Night Football. But I walked in to find that all of Gloria's things were gone. I was shocked to say the least and when she drove up with her loaded car, she got out and told me that she really didn't like Denver and was moving back to Tennessee. Wow.

"Patti, you knew I didn't like it here. I've been homesick and besides, you knew about the wedding I was going to go to back home in the fall. I didn't really plan on living here for long; I just wanted to check it out for a while. You knew that," she told me.

Well I didn't know that, and I've never known anyone to take their microwave on a sight-seeing trip to Colorado, but that's what Gloria did. I sure didn't enjoy the Broncos game as planned and when she left in the morning, I was not thrilled about the situation I was in, with rent and all. She had left me in a bad situation and we weren't the best of friends for quite a while, but it's just not worth it to let those angry feelings get in the way of friendship. We eventually talked it out and we've been friends again for years. Thank goodness!

So Jesse and I lived in the house until three more months of the six-month lease was up. I approached my wonderful landlords and asked them to please release me from the lease. They did. They understood what had happened and were very gracious to me. I had some fantastic friends at Chad's, where I now worked full time and one of them, Trudee, offered us a place to stay until I knew what I was doing.

Chapter 25

What I was doing, was trying to find a place to live in up in the mountains. Even though it was a bad time of the year for doing this, I thought I'd try. In the meantime, Jesse and I lived with Trudee, Mike and their son Ryan. Jesse and I lived in the basement apartment and it worked out very well. We tried to maintain a low profile, but they invited us to join them upstairs all the time. They had a large back yard where Jesse could run around, and she spent a good deal of time outside barking at the winds that carried a great variety of scents from the foothills of the mountains. She certainly enjoyed the new space, and they liked having Jesse around, but Trudee worried when Jesse occasionally snuck out of the back yard and played in the front yard. But I always told Trudee that if Jesse ever got out on the street in front of a car, it wasn't her fault because Jesse knew she was supposed to stay in the back, especially when there was plenty of room, but she just preferred front yards and hated to feel left out of the action.

Well, one day she had plenty of action. I had been up in Vail visiting a friend and looking for a place to live. I arrived home late in the afternoon and just put a foot outside my truck stepping down, when Ryan ran out of the house shouting, "Patti! Jesse ran away this morning and we can't find her! She's gone!"

"Ryan! I said I would tell her." Trudee came walking towards me with a very worried look on her kind face. "Oh Patti. I let her out this morning and she must have jumped the fence. I went to let her in and she was gone. We looked all over the neighborhood, but there was no sign of her. I'm so sorry. I'm so sorry. I don't know what to do."

"Trudee." I gave her a hug, then stepped back and tried to console this poor woman who was beside herself with worry over my renegade dog. "Remember what I have always told you? If anything ever happens to Jesse, it is not your fault. Jesse jumps fences and there's nothing I can do about it. She's a regular gazelle—I don't how she does it." I tried to lighten up the situation and show Trudee that I truly didn't blame her, because I didn't. I knew how Jesse was and had lived with it for six years by now. She wasn't what I would call an athletic dog, but when it came to confinement her motto was "Don't fence me in." Period. We walked back into the house and I kept reiterating the fact that it wasn't Trudee's fault. I went out looking for Jesse in the short time left before dark, and said that I'd look in the morning too—she'll show up.

But she didn't. I went out looking for her for hours, first thing in the morning, but there was no sign of her. It was Sunday, so I watched football during the afternoon, and tried to get my mind off the fact that Jesse was gone. Knowing that the leash laws in Colorado were quite strict, I sincerely hoped and believed that she had been picked up by Animal Control. But still, every half hour or so, I ventured outside; hoping to see any sign of her. At one point I passed a young guy walking on the side of the street and asked him, "Hey, have you seen a big white dog anywhere?"

"No I haven't. Have you seen a small black cat anywhere?" He asked me, quietly laughing at the irony.

"No I haven't, sorry," I answered, chuckling with him.

Sunday dragged on and on. I couldn't call the shelters because they were closed on the weekends, so I was going to have to wait until the morning. Trudee came home from work and was visibly upset when she saw that the big white ghost had really disappeared. I was doing my best to appear hopeful about the situation and not be upset in Trudee's presence, but when I went to bed that night without Jesse by my side, not knowing where she was, for the second night in a row, I cried myself to sleep.

I had to wait until nine a.m. to reach any shelters, and I called every one on the west side of town, as well as any in Denver proper. I was trying not to think of the possibility that someone would steal her, as I had been warned about in the past, or that she was a road pancake somewhere. She'll be at a shelter I kept telling myself—and Trudee too. I was finally able to get through to the Lakewood shelter and they said they might have a dog fitting that description, but they didn't think so. We agreed that I should come and see for myself because people have been known to label breeds differently, especially in the retriever section of the dog world. I told Trudee that I'd call her at work when I found anything out.

During the drive to the shelter in the unpredicted snowstorm that slowed the traffic, I tried to control my roller-coaster emotions. Trying not to be too hopeful, but begging she would be there, I wiped my tears away and walked inside. The lady told me to go in and walk the aisles to see if my dog was there. My throat tightened at the sight of the first dog as it looked up at me with such hope in its eyes. As I continued up and down the rows of large cages that contained sadly howling dogs, I couldn't stop the tears—crying for the animals, crying for Jesse, and crying for myself. When I was on the last of the four rows of cages, with only three cages left to inspect, I blinked through the river of tears, looked into a cage and saw four white paws lazily stretched out on the concrete floor.

"Jesse?!" I exclaimed.

She opened her eyes and looked up at me with surprise, then jumped up from her relaxed position and started wagging her entire body far more than I had ever seen her do when greeting me. She was so very happy to see me and I was over-joyed.

"Hi Mom! What took you so long?" she asked as she was wriggling and jiggling all over the cage.

"Oh Jesse, it's you! It's you!" I couldn't believe it! I found her! It was one of the happiest moments of my life.

The fact that she had jumped the fence, ran around the neighborhood and had been caught by the dog police was completely immaterial at that point. I opened the cage door and we had a wonderful reunion. Jesse was jumping all over me, actually licking my face (she never did that), and I was hugging her fiercely and crying with tears of utter joy. She was safe and we were together again.

I walked to the office door with Jesse jumping up and down by my side. I opened it and we walked through together. The lady jumped up and yelled at me, "Ma'am, you're not supposed to let the dog out of the cage."

"But it's her! It's my dog!" I exclaimed happily, bending to pet and hug Jesse.

"I'm sorry, but she'll have to go in here," and she whisked Jesse away and put her into a room by herself. Jesse immediately jumped up, put her paws on the glass, looked right at me and howled very loudly. She was confused. I looked back at her. I was confused.

Then the lady told me. "You have to do all the paperwork and pay all the charges, before you can have your dog."

Not a problem. Luckily they took Visa. Weekend jail is expensive.

During the time I was bringing Jesse into the room, there was a young man who found his Irish setter there and was doing his paperwork. We chatted about our pets and how glad we were that they were safe and how we found them, but when he pulled out his American Express card, he was out of luck. They didn't take it. The lady was processing the release forms for Jesse and immediately I thought, "Bring your hope and bring their leash, but leave your American Express card at home, because at the Lakewood Animal Shelter, we don't take American Express. Visa, it's everywhere you want to be." It just ran through my head in an instant. Been watching too much football on TV. I didn't want him to leave without his dog and wanted to help, so I offered to put his bill on my credit card and he could get the cash at a bank, but then he found his Visa. We were comrades in the despair-turned-to-happiness department of emotions. He was grateful to me and I was glad he was getting his dog.

We said good bye and I loaded Jesse into the truck and headed to Chad's to see Trudee. I knew she'd be extremely relieved. When Trudee came outside with me to see the jailbird, Jesse hopped out of the cab of the truck and was jumping all around the parking lot like a kangaroo trying to play with Trudee, who was laughing and hugging me and jumping around herself with happiness and relief. She turned to Jesse, pointed a finger at the jumping goofball and told her, "You better not ever do that again, young lady! I was worried sick." So Trudee went back to work, I took Jesse home, and Trudee never had to worry about Jesse again. We moved back to Denver.

Chapter 26

I had tried to find a place to live in the mountains, but just couldn't at that time of year. Not meant to be I guess. When I returned to work from yet another house-searching trip to Vail, I saw Carolyn (who also worked at Chad's) sitting at the back table taking a break. "Hi Carolyn, how's it going?" I asked as I sat down.

"Great. How was your trip to Vail, did you find anything?" She wondered.

"No, I didn't. It's really the wrong time to be looking. Either everything's taken, or it's absolutely outrageously priced." I grinned despondently.

"Well, if you'll wait until this fall, I'll move up there with you."

"Really? You want to move up there too?" I asked in surprise.

"Well, I don't like Vail, but I'd move to Summit County, if you want to go there," she offered. Summit County was just east of Vail over the pass, more laid-back, affordable and had a variety of communities.

"Yeah, that'd be great! I really didn't like Vail either, but that's where my friend lived and I thought it'd be easier if I knew someone who lived there. But if you'll move up to the mountains too, sure!" I returned her smile and we shook hands on it.

In the meantime, I found a wonderful older house for Jesse and myself. It was close to my old neighborhood by the lake, on a very quiet street. We had a roomy and comfortable garden apartment, complete with low hanging pipes that 12 (I counted) firemen could hit their helmet-clad heads on when they hurried into the apartment carrying axes and tanks, after they had driven way too many noisy ladder trucks to come and check out the bubbling and hissing coming from my ancient furnace at 1:00 in the morning. (The neighbors weren't happy with the new girl on the block.) As I stood listening to the chief explain what I should do to release the pressure, I discretely counted all the cute men standing around, and thought they must have been really bored that night to go through this much commotion for one old furnace.

We had a fenced in yard and the whole place to ourselves. It was very convenient for me to let Jesse out. I just had to open my door and she was confined. It was the perfect set up for us and we enjoyed the new living arrangement.

One balmy night in late January, I returned home from work with an armload of groceries. I let Jesse out, went inside, unpacked the groceries and sat to watch TV in my jammies, while recovering from a busy night. I sat and relaxed and was content in the world of unwinding, when I began to wonder why Jesse hadn't knocked to come in. I walked over to the door, opened it and was shocked. The steps were covered with a few inches of snow. Wow! It was warm out when I came in. It wasn't supposed to snow at all, much less accumulate.

I have since learned; you don't believe what the weather forecasters say in Colorado. The mountains create their own weather. One time, a man I was waiting on asked why we didn't get the predicted fourteen inches of snow that day. I didn't know and he said, "I'd sure like to make over fifty thousand dollars a year and never have to be right." Poor mountain area weather forecasters. I'm sure they have to be right sometimes, but I bet that their percentage of prediction accuracy is lower than the national average.

So, not only was it a surprise to see all the snow, it was a surprise to see that I had accidentally left the gate open and Jesse was gone. Oh, no, not again. Half angry at myself for being so stupid, I quickly grabbed my purple bubble coat—you know, those great warm Michelin Man looking coats from the 70's and 80's—and put it on over my pajamas. I wrapped my scarf around my neck, stepped into my big boots and headed out into the heavily falling snow. I walked into the front yard, figuring that was the way she had to go and quickly realized that her large paws left big marks in the snow. Great! I could just follow her tracks and catch up with her. So up the street I went, saying hi to the man who was getting a head start on the morning shoveling chore. I asked him if he had seen a big white dog. No, he hadn't. I continued up the street and turned the corner following the tracks.

Jesse had gone back into the alley and was meandering around the garages, the garbage cans and the laneways of every house she came to. The tracks looked like the chutes on a chutes-and-ladder game board, going from here to there and all over the place. I kept tracking her for about a half an hour; through alleys, up and down streets, in tons of laneways and all around the neighborhood. I was crossing another street, when I realized that the snow, which was now falling with a vengeance, was filling in the tracks faster than I could follow them. "How stupid is this?" I thought out loud to myself as I stood up straight. "I'm in the middle of a whiteout, looking for a white dog, it's dumping tons of snow now, I'm losing the tracks, it's midnight and I'm in my pajamas. This is really dumb. The heck with this." I turned towards home, but followed what I thought were tracks through the alley. One more shot at tracking her down. I looked up from my misguided diligence and barely saw through the snow that I was in my alley. I walked towards the fence of my back yard, and who was sitting there at the top of the steps, with a white hat of snow on her white furry head, looking right at me? Yup. Jesse. She had apparently been there for a while—judging from the size of her snow hat. I was really glad she was safe, but was mad at her for making me track her all around the neighborhood at midnight for nothing. Animal Control seemed to be a daylight job. I let her in and went to bed.

Jesse and I enjoyed having the whole house to ourselves until one Sunday afternoon, a guy named Bob came by to look at the upstairs apartment for his brother, himself and his female shepherd-Husky mix named Indigo. Bob and I hit it off immediately, but I told him we'd have to make sure that the girls would get along, before we sealed the deal. I was a bit concerned about the Husky factor. I drove him to get Indigo, and when I saw her, I was astonished. She had the most incredible crystal blue eyes I had ever seen on a dog. They seemed to actually glow, from the blackness of the fur that lined her beautiful face. She was friendly to me and I liked her right away, hoping Jesse would feel the same.

We loaded Indigo into the truck and brought her back to the house. We watched as the two dogs sniffed and walked lightly around each , as we talked to them with soft voices and hopeful hearts. They weren't best friends right away, but since Indigo was a much younger dog, Jesse liked her and took a slightly motherly role from the beginning, which was fine with Indigo but ironic. Indigo had a litter of pups at a young age, so she was really the mom while Jesse just acted like one. Soon they became best friends and they'd sit out in the yard all day long and share stories. Jesse listened to Indigo tell her about having all the kids and Jesse told Indigo about her many travels.

During the time I've spent in Ireland, I've found that Irish dogs are either really smart or they truly have the luck of the Irish while they are out and about. And I've seen dogs out walking themselves all the time. Up and down the street they go, not just sitting by the pub where their master is having a pint, but checking out the sights and smells of their village. One day I watched a dog as she was crossing the road. She looked to her side when she was in the center and hesitated to let the speeding car that would have turned her into a road pancake, pass her. I've actually seen this a few times here and don't remember seeing this behavior in the States, where sometimes dogs unfortunately end up motionless, on the side of the road. It seems these Irish dogs are pretty good at the art of self-walking.

Since Jesse took herself on walks either at night when I couldn't catch up to her, or during the day when the Animal Control people are out and about, I had never seen her walking down the street by herself. But maybe there was an Irish setter lurking behind those retriever eyes. One night Bob and I were driving home from shooting pool, and in the near distance we saw a large white dog, cruising down the usually very busy Sheridan Avenue. "Hey Patti, look at that dog taking itself for a walk." Bob laughed as he pointed.

"Yeah, silly dog. I th... HEY! It's Jesse! Oh my gosh!" I shouted. Suddenly nervous for her safety, I whipped the truck across the right lane, swerved to the curb and put the flashers on. I was really glad that there hadn't been a car in the lane—I would have taken them out like a stock car. I had reacted so suddenly without a thought for our safety. Bob hopped out of the truck and called Jesse.

She came bounding over. "Hi you guys! What are you doing here?"

"What are YOU doing here is the real question."

"Just out walking Mom. It's a nice night and I was bored."

"Not a good idea Jesse. It's a busy street and you could have been hit by a car!"

"But I was on the sidewalk."

"Don't get cute, Jess. Get in the truck young lady."

We put her in the back of the truck and took her home. I had a very long talk with her about taking herself for walks and as far as I know, she never did again while we lived in Denver.

Chapter 27

We enjoyed our summer living in Denver. It was very hot but it was dry, so it wasn't nearly as uncomfortable as the heat and humidity of Nashville. Jesse was happy we lived in Colorado. She didn't pant all day long, or scratch at insect bites like she did when we lived in Tennessee. We didn't have a good swimming lake nearby, but we did have a five foot big turtle shaped green kiddie pool. It was fabulous. My pals and I used to sit around in a circle and put our feet in the cold water to break the heat on those hot summer days. Jesse would sometimes get into the pool and lie down, causing a premature pool break in order for me to use my nylon-over-a-hanger pool scooper to scoop out all the white fur that floated on the water. I'd whistle then shout, "Everyone out of the pool." My buddies would remove their feet, I'd clean the water, and we'd resume our foot-cooling delight.

I had changed jobs in order to work closer to home. Now I worked at Marlowe's on the 16th Avenue Mall in the heart of Denver. I could ride my bike to work and really liked the restaurant and the people there, but I still visited with my pals from Chad's. Carolyn and I still talked about moving up to the mountains, but we didn't have any concrete plans yet.

One night I went into Chad's, saw Carolyn sitting at the stand up bar and sat down to join her. I had recently met some people from Alaska, and after looking at the article on whale migration in my National Geographic magazine, I decided that I wanted to go to Alaska in the spring. "Hey Carolyn, what are you doing next May?" I asked her.

"I don't know, why?" she said, a bit puzzled.

"Do you want to go to Alaska?" I blurted out to her.

"Alaska? What do you mean?"

"Last week I met some really cool people from Alaska and I want to go and see the whales. Do you wanna go?"

"Yeah, sure." she said, without even a thimble full of hesitation. She smiled and we shook hands. It might have been risky to ask someone whom I really didn't know that well to go on this trip, but somehow I knew it was all right.

Summer floated by and on October 1, 1988, we moved up to Frisco in Summit County as planned and we both found jobs at Copper Mountain ski resort. We were all adjusting to the new living arrangement that was quite different for me 'n Jess. Carolyn had two cats. Gato; a gorgeous calico with a lights-are-on-but-nobody-home look about her, and her daughter Bandit; a stunning torte cat who either sat like a porcelain statue and glared at Jesse, or ran away when Jesse wanted to play. Jesse had kitty friends in the past and loved cats, but these two weren't fond of this large and foreign white annoyance who disrupted their little kitty world. But we soon settled into a friendly and tolerant group of females living together and enjoying the beauty, adventures, and activities that the mountains offered.

After our first extremely busy and hectic winter season of working in restaurants in a ski resort—which can deplete your patience for any type of customer, much less the tourists, we were excited to have a long trip ahead of us.

On May 1, 1989, we headed to Denver to catch the highway to Cheyenne and were on our way north to Alaska. We started the six thousand mile trip with a rag stuffed into the gas hole on the side of the truck because when I filled up the gas tank in Denver, I accidentally left the gas cap at the station. It looked lovely and added a touch of class. We pulled off the highway in Billings, Montana to try to find a gas cap, and the store ended up being the CARQUEST headquarters for the West. I bought two caps. Just in case. It was a stroke of good luck. A good sign for the trip.

I had some friends from Tennessee, Debbie and Glen, who had moved to Bozeman a few years earlier, and we stayed with them for a couple of days. Their two girls, Nicole and Shay, absolutely fell in love with Jesse and they sat with her constantly, petting and talking to her all day long. I was happy that she was so comfortable with children, although I never had reason to worry. Remember, she was the live book of things to do for kids. I know that golden retrievers are famous for their high tolerance level, but I have heard of shepherds with short fuses and was pleased that Jesse sided with the retriever half of her personality and enjoyed the attentions of young 'uns.

When we left Bozeman and were headed to Alberta, it was the first time we were driving in Montana on a sunny day. I don't know the scientific reason why, but the sky there truly is BIG. Just like the license plates say. Living in Colorado, we see plenty of wide-open spaces and views that go on forever, but Montana has something special. Maybe it's the curvature of the earth, maybe it's the imagination, I don't know, but when we looked up at that sky, it stretched on forever and ever. We couldn't help ourselves from stopping and getting out of the truck, just to look up and marvel at the sky. I'm sure Montana folks are accustomed to seeing people standing in the middle of the road staring up at their sky. They probably have some cute name for it, like... idiot.

As we drew closer to the border of Alberta, the sky still seemed big, but in a different way. Strange. The small town of Sweet Grass was where we had our first of many border crossings. As some Americans know, the Canadian government is extremely strict about firearms, with zero tolerance for bucking their system. The border guard asked us, "Do you have any firearms of any kind with you?"

"No we don't," I nervously answered her.

"Are you aware that in Canada, firearms and handguns of any kind are illegal according to the law outlined in... so I will ask you again, do you have any firearms of any kind with you?" She was very exacting in her speech and questioning, thinking we were hiding something because of my nervous mannerisms.

"No. We don't. Jesse here is our only weapon, but don't tell anyone she doesn't have all her teeth," I seriously told the lady, who chuckled at my comment and let us go on our way.

Even though Jesse was not yet seven years old, she had lost a few of her teeth. I was told it was probably due to having mange. Luckily the missing teeth were not in the front, so she could still look vicious if need be.

We decided that Carolyn would handle the rest of the border crossings because I was too nervous about them. I'm a Canadian citizen, but I was so concerned about getting Jesse's paperwork in order, that I forgot about mine and I was afraid of being held up forever or fined, so from then on, I just smiled and nodded from the passenger's seat.

We wanted to stop before getting to Calgary so we looked for a place to camp way back in the boonies. We took what we finally realized was a missed turn and found the place, but in our moments of being lost, we saw an incredible sight. A massive bull elk was standing on the edge of an outcropping and was silhouetted against the pink and purple and orange hues of the setting sun. The road we were on was fairly close to where he towered over us, but he didn't even move. He just stood there watching us and we were in heaven. It was absolutely majestic.

When we finally reached our first Canadian campground, which was west of Nanton, it was getting dark, so we set up camp and headed to bed. It had been a long day.

We woke up to see that we had found a wonderfully peaceful spot with spectacular views of the Canadian Rockies in the distance. There was a small dam that created some beautiful little lakes that were all joined together and they reflected the mountains to make some fantastic panoramas. It made sense. We found out later that our first of many campgrounds in Canada was a Provincial Park called Chain Lakes.

We said good bye to this grand place and while we were on the gravel road on our way back to the main highway, we ran into a father and son who were driving cattle towards their ranch. Jesse traveled in the back, in the confines of the shell and saw the masses of cattle strolling by. She started barking up a storm, and was trying to get at them through the skinny camper windows. The father, riding point, started chuckling and asked, "Hey, can I borrow your dog?"

"Oh you wouldn't want her. She'd run those cattle all over creation," I answered him smiling.

"She sure wants to get at them, doesn't she?" He grinned, "What kind is she?"

"Half golden retriever, half white shepherd."

"Not exactly a cattle dog, eh?" He laughed, nodded, tipped his hat and moved on down the road.

When we came to the son riding drag, he stopped, tipped his hat and asked, "Where're you ladies coming from?"

"We were camping back there," I pointed back towards the campsite area. "Is that where you live?"

"Yup. Have a place back up that way. Where're you from? Where're you headed?"

"We're from Colorado, and we're on our way to Alaska."

"Oowee! Really? All by yourselves? Alaska? That sure is a long ways away." He was surprised.

We sat and chatted briefly and he said that it was too bad we were in a hurry, because he would have invited us up to the house for a coffee. I really don't know how we gave the impression that we were in a hurry, because we weren't. I guess it was because we had such a long trip ahead of us. We reluctantly said bye and headed on up the road, putting in a John Denver tape and singing, "Think I'd Rather Be A Cowboy" at the top of our lungs. We wished that we would have taken the time to see the ranch and maybe even go for a ride. I sometimes wonder how that day would have turned out if we had said sure, we'll go. We're not in a hurry. Carpe Diem, seize the moment.

Chapter 28

The moment I saw the full moon out in front of me as I was speeding towards Dublin, I knew that I'd enjoy the drive, despite being exhausted. It was 5:45 a.m. when I started the long journey to pick up my mom from the airport. It had been Friday the thirteenth, with a full moon the night before, and now I was in a very sedate mood. I said farewell to the man who had a strong hold on my heart and left behind a place that for me, held a magical appeal unlike any place I had ever been.

As I flew by the rolling fields and peaceful farms of Northern Ireland, I was in awe. The soft light of the rising sun was touching the lingering mist in the fields and heavy fog that was rising from the valleys, while the bright full moon was smiling away in the western sky. The animals were waking up and leisurely moving around in their lush green fields. Some were high on the ridges, and their gray silhouettes against the delicately layered orange and blue-hued sky created some magnificent scenes. I was thankful for these views, because my jumbled mind was able to drink in the picturesque and peaceful sights. I felt like I was in a twilight zone, such was the mixture of emotions flowing through my veins. It's very strange to feel numb and full of adrenaline at the same moment in time.

I made it to the airport safely and relatively on time and immediately found my mom by the information desk. "Hi Mum! I'm so glad you're safe and sound. How was the flight?" I asked as I hugged her with great relief that I found her, since we hadn't had a predetermined meeting place.

"Hi, honey! It was wonderful. Everyone was so very pleasant and friendly, I loved it." She smiled a semi-tired smile.

"So what do you want to do, where do you want to go?" I asked, already having tentatively planned to go south, to some areas like Waterford and Cork that I thought she'd really enjoy.

"I want to go to Northern Ireland and to the north of regular Ireland."

"But I can't go back there!" I exclaimed in tired panic, as I instinctively stepped backward, hearing B's words in my mind.

"What do you mean you can't go back there?" She drew closer to me with concern all over her face.

"I just can't go back there, Mum." I tried to calm myself.

"What's wrong? What have you done?"

My poor mother. Worried as she was, I had to tell her.

"I met a guy up there." I grew quiet. I was too whipped to say anymore.

"So? Did you do something that you can't see him again or don't you want to?" She was thoroughly confused and I didn't blame her. This ragged and weary daughter of hers was acting like an escaped convict.

"No, Mum. The first thing I want to do is turn right around and go to see him again," I admitted to her.

"Why don't we get out of here and we can talk about it," she wisely suggested.

So I drove to the Dublin pier. I don't really know why I chose it, but it was a peaceful spot and was what I desperately needed at the time. While we had a snack, I told Mum the whole story about Danny. She was intrigued to say the least. This story was coming from her over-forty-year-old daughter, who has maintained a very single life all along and was now hooked on this Irish fisherman. I think it was a mixture of curiosity, understanding and desire to go north that led my mom to say, "Then let's go back." I couldn't even believe my ears. Wait until I tell B!

I called Sean and told him the news. He wasn't sure if he should believe me, when I said I had absolutely NOT prompted Mum to want to go there. He was full at the B&B that night, so we just drove around and up through Belfast and stayed in Cushendun. It worked out great and we had a good night's sleep.

We awoke that Sunday to gorgeous weather. It was a perfect day to drive around and observe the stunning views that the eastern coast of Northern Ireland has to offer. It seemed that everyone was out doing the same, which created a lot of traffic that I had to get around, and it took forever to get to Greenane, but I stayed calm because I wanted Mum to enjoy the sights, the beautiful day and the fact that we were in Ireland together. Yippee!

I was in a fog, due to the fact that I might see Danny yet again. It amazed me how crazy I was about this man and how crazy the whole story was. What was it about him that had me all tied up in knots, and how could I fall so hard? Never in my life, had anything remotely this unimaginable, ever happened to me. It was like something you read about in a fiction novel. But it seemed that fate repeatedly stepped in, creating chances for me to see him.

I had asked Sean to please tell Danny that I was coming back, but he didn't get the chance. So Danny had no idea I was going to be in the small village of Greenane that afternoon, when he was strolling down the street on the way to O'Malley's. Fate. I drove past him, caught my breath and said, "Oh my gosh! That was Danny!" I whipped the car around, went back, stopped across the road from him and said, "Hey!"

He looked at me, smiled and sauntered over to the car. I introduced Mum and we all chatted for a few moments, while my heart was pounding away once again. I told him we'd see him shortly and we headed to the B&B, where Sean, Tim, Mum and I had a quick cuppa tea.

It had started to rain as soon as Mum and I headed out to walk the shore path to town, and we were soaked when we arrived at O'Malley's. So much for fixing the hair. I ordered a pint for each of us, and we joined Danny at the table by the window. It was lucky we had bumped into him on the street because now, it wouldn't be a shock for him to see us walk into the pub. I knew he was in shock anyway, because this crazy girl was here to see him again.

There were some friendly people sitting right next to us and between them, myself and Danny, Mum had plenty of conversations going on. She spent time talking to Danny about fishing and things and she liked him too. We stayed at the pub for a while and enjoyed the evening.

Because we were sitting on the end of the group, sometimes Danny and I were able to talk privately about some things I wanted to know about him and the things I wanted to tell him. It was a meaningful conversation about some important issues, but we also had some good laughs. When he got up to leave, I told him that I wanted to say goodbye to him outside. I was getting used to saying bye to him and yet never wanted to.

When we were finally able to say the last goodbye, he headed off down the street with his pal Liam and I slowly headed back into the pub to rejoin Mum. I had just sat down, when I jumped up and exclaimed, "The tape!"

On that rainy evening, on Friday the 13, when Danny and I were driving around during the full moon, I liked the tape we were listening to and asked him who it was. He told me who and said that I could have it, but I forgot to get it from him. I jokingly told him this Sunday night that I came back just to get the tape. Umm hmmm sure.

I ran out the door, down the street, around the corner and saw the dark shapes slowly walking up the road. I whistled loudly and hollered, "The tape!" Running to catch up to them, I joined them and walked arm in arm with Danny to get the precious tape.

Standing outside his house after I had the tape, we talked and had a long goodbye all over again. It was too much. I didn't want to walk away, but I had to. "I will never, ever, forget you, Danny." I told him with all my heart, as I looked up into the face that would forever be etched in my mind.

"Promise?" He smiled.

"Yes. I promise." He turned and I watched him as he slowly walked into his house, all too familiar with the feelings I was experiencing yet again. I stood for a moment, and then ran down the road back to the pub (thanking God that I could run), sat down and tried to catch my breath while I told Mum that I had it. I had the tape. The Wolf Tones Millennium tape.

A sunny day in the Yukon.

Chapter 29

The only wolf we saw on our Alaska trip was in the Yukon, on the wall of The Full Moon Saloon. It was an antique pelt from a wolf that someone shot in the early 1900's. It was massive and in pretty good shape. It's not that we weren't in areas where wolves lived, we just didn't see them. But we did see some gorgeous foxes and a few black bears that were moseying around in the woods.

One night we stayed in a campground near Watson Lake and were the only humans around for miles. It was early in the season and most of the campgrounds where we stayed were not open yet, but we figured that if they weren't blocked and we were able to get in, why not stay. While we were sitting playing cribbage, the ranger drove by, said howdy (not asking us to pay, which we would have), waved and went on his way—so we knew it was OK for us to be there.

Usually when we weren't in areas that were prone to bears, I slept in the truck with Jesse, while Carolyn slept in a tent nearby. Otherwise, Carolyn and I slept in the back of the truck in our sleeping bags nestled amongst the backpacks, and Jesse comfortably slept in the cab on her blanket. It was a good arrangement that allowed all of us a peaceful sleep. But in the middle of this night, out in the middle of nowhere, we woke up to hear what sounded like metal scraping on metal. I whispered to Carolyn, "What's that?"

"I don't know." She answered, as we didn't move a muscle, lying like a couple of sardines in a can.

In a split second, my mind flashed the image of a gigantic grizzly bear, rearing on his hind legs with his mouth contorted as he snarled and growled at us. His massive paws were pawing at our scents in the air that he detected with his keen nose and he was going to rip us all to shreds.

"Do you think it's a bear?" I wondered out loud.

"I don't know, but I don't think so."

The image snapped to gray and my heart slowed its frantic beating as my imagination was overcome with the reality that we were hopefully very safe in our little brown metal cocoon, and whatever was making those scary sounds would quickly and calmly move away from the vehicle.

"Maybe we should look and see." I timidly suggested.

"I'm not getting up to see."

"Then I'm not getting up to see." I chimed in, briefly remembering my vision. We stayed there—stiff, silent and listening, and soon decided it wasn't anything to worry about. So we rolled over and went back to sleep—until we were rudely awakened by the blare of some kind of horn.

"What's that?" we asked each in unison.

"I don't know," I answered our question.

"Sounds like a horn."

"Yeah, it does."

"Who would be beeping a horn at this time of night?" Carolyn, asked, slightly annoyed.

"I don't know. I didn't think there was anyone else here," I mumbled to her, also displeased at the second interruption of my slumber.

"I didn't either."

"Well, it couldn't be us," I said in my sleepy cobwebbed state of mind and rolled over to go back to sleep.

"Yeah I know it's not us, but I wonder who it is. Oh well." Carolyn also wrote off the annoying noise. But it wasn't long until she said, "Patti, wake up. It's still there. We have to see what's happening."

"OK." We sat up, trying to be awake, thought for a minute and opened the back window to climb out. Now that I could hear the outside noises, I realized that it was us! I crawled out and walked to the driver's side of the truck, saw inside the cab and started cracking up. "Hey Carolyn, I found the problem!" I shouted to her through my laughter.

Jesse usually slept quietly, but she must have had some bad dreams this night. I could tell from the ruffled blanket that she had shifted her body around a lot. At one point, she must have bumped the large bag of dog food and it fell against the horn, pushing on it, keeping it blaring loudly. I went around to let Jesse out for a while—the poor girl with the horn in her ears— and I set the bag of food in a position where this couldn't happen again. Carolyn and I had a hard time going back to sleep this time, because we were too busy laughing at ourselves. "Oh, no, it couldn't possibly be us. How could it be us? Oh, no, it's not us." What a pair of imbeciles. We were the only ones around for miles.

Jesse enjoyed this Alaskan trip because she had a place to call her own where she watched everything go whizzing by. She had the freedom to go safely all over the bed of the truck and she barked to her heart's content. She usually scared away the wildlife that would be close to the truck, so we were glad that the windows were completely caked with mud when we saw the magnificent caribou on the Denali Highway.

Someone told us that this highway cutting across the center of the state had just opened two days before. So we decided we would take that much shorter route to Denali National Park instead of going all the way down to Anchorage and back up again, which would have added a few hundred miles to the trip.

We headed out on the most incredible section of roadway that we had seen so far. A beautiful black ribbon of asphalt, painted with bright white sidelines, crisp yellow centerlines; wide and roomy blacktop, gently curving and snaking its way along in front of the stunning Alaskan Mountain Range. It was a welcome sight and we couldn't stop marveling. (The Alcan Highway however is an adventure in driving all on its own. With potholes that can swallow a VW Bug with hardly a burp, frost heaves that will make you wish you had a helmet on when your head crashes into the roof of the truck, and narrow curves that would shake up a NASCAR driver, it's certainly a unique experience.) So, singing a happy road song and loving life, we traveled down this carefree highway. We drove a mere twenty miles, when we saw it in the distance. It seemed to loom over the road. As we approached it, we knew it was the one. That dreaded sign: Pavement Ends. It confronted us; big, bright, orange, and depressing. It was a familiar enemy. In an instant, this road turned into the absolute worst road of the trip and we were having our very own nightmare in the middle of the day. It took us five hours to go 115 miles along a muddy track, that we slip-slided slowly along frontwards, sideways and almost backwards at times. After about three hours, I felt that we were truly in the wrong twilight zone. No commercials. No commentator. No chance of survival.

When we happened upon the caribou, Jesse was wrapped in darkness because of the mud slathered windows, so she had no idea they were there. Happy that I could get fairly close, I was able to snap some good photos. I took the time to stretch and look around at the monochromatic beauty of the snow-dusted mountains, the cloud-screened sun giving off its satin light and the grazing animals. It was a treat to see these sights and served to lessen my frustration caused by the bumpy, muddy, endless track of road we were trapped on. After this welcome break, we bumped along for a couple more hours, and then found a bar near the Denali National Park to quench our thirst and let my truck rest.

My poor truck. I felt very bad for my little truck that had safely carried us this far without any problems. Before we left for our trip, Carolyn had suggested a few ideas she heard from people who had been on the Alcan, so I had taken precautions to protect certain vital organs of my truck, one being hardware cloth wrapped around the radiator. We figured out that the noise we heard that night at Watson Lake was probably a por-cupine eating the dead bugs off the wire mesh. Hardly a bear. Even though we survived the Denali Highway, I ended up having to put new shocks on my truck when we were in Anchorage. It was amazing that the exact shocks I needed were there. Someone had put in a special order, but they never showed up to claim them. Lucky, lucky, lucky.

We took that shortcut across the Denali Highway because we were going to go into the Denali National Park before heading down to Anchorage and stay with some of Carolyn's friends from Minnesota, but decided against it because of weather. Jimmy and Joy had moved to Alaska years before, and when Carolyn called them to ask about a visit, they were very excited. They even suggested that we come skiing with them on the Ruth Glacier at the base of Denali (Mt. McKinley). Since we didn't want to be under pressure to have to be in Anchorage by a certain time to catch a plane to go with them, we said we'd just meet them in Anchorage. Besides, we had Jesse with us and what would we do with her when we were skiing?

So after spending the night at the campground that was conveniently located beside the bar we found, we headed for Anchorage. When we saw the signs for Talkeetna we had to make a decision. The man who had told us about the Denali Highway also told us that it was worth it to take a flight around Mt. McKinley. He also said that if we mentioned his name to his friend Jim at K2 Airline Company, we would get a good deal on a flight. Do we do it? What would we do with Jesse? Oh what the heck let's go and take a look.

We found K2 and met Jim. He offered us a great deal, so I asked the lady in the office if she wouldn't mind keeping an eye on Jesse while we were up and away. She said sure, no problem and asked me to tie Jesse to the post on the front porch. I sat with Jesse for a bit, told her that we would be back in a while and left her food and water bowls with her. She understood "back in a while", a phrase she had heard frequently, so I wasn't too concerned.

She knew that phrase, but she didn't know what happened to her mom when she watched me disappear into the sky. When we talked to the lady at the base, she said, "Tell the girl that her dog broke the rope and took off running after the plane, but I ran out and caught her. She's here with me and she's fine now."

Oops. I didn't think Jesse would do that. I thought that she'd do the bark-in-a-quick-fit-of-anger-then-lay-down-and-watch-for-me-thing, like she always did. Either she really did love me or it was the abandonment issue again.

Flying around the glaciers was one of the coolest adventures I have ever experienced. The views were spectacular and the sensation of flying in a small aircraft so closely to the mountains and glaciers was thrilling. The landing was more than thrilling however, as we were pitched and tossed in the strong winds like a torn-up kite with a broken tail. Jim the pilot said that the landing conditions were amongst the top three worst ones he had ever seen. Splendid. But we landed safely, albeit white knuckled. After spending time walking around and absorbing the magnificence of the glacier and observing the spectacular blue light that seems to shine from the depths of the ice, we departed to go back to the office. But Jim got a call. He turned and asked us if we minded that he had to stop at the Ruth Glacier to pick someone up. Are you kidding? We'd have to fly around longer? No problem. Carolyn looked at me with a gleam in her eye and I knew exactly what she was thinking. That would be great!

We had a better landing on the Ruth, and when we hopped out of the plane, a guy came skiing by. We asked him if he knew any of the people that were in the various camps and he started pointing and naming off the groups. "These people are from Anchorage, those way over there are from Japan, those guys up there are from National Geographic. They're shooting some film or something, I'm not sure, and those there (the camp right in front of us, a little more than a quarter of a mile away) are also from Anchorage."

We could see movement, so Carolyn shouted to them calling their name. Low and behold, a moment later a lady came out and shouted, "Tut! Tut! Is that you?" Joy ran through the snow towards Carolyn, who was also running, and the two of them fell together laughing and rolling around in the snow of the Ruth Glacier. It was pretty amazing to incidentally meet Jimmy and Joy on a glacier in Alaska. It was totally unplanned and ironic to say the least. I love when that happens!

"Pretty nice place you have here, nice to meet you," was what I said to the wonderfully fun couple who let us stay with them in Anchorage for a week. They showed us around the area, we explored new places together and they even fed us moose ribs. Yummy.

🦴 🦴 🦴

Chapter 30

Moose are extremely territorial animals and you don't ever want to challenge them about this fact. But they also have poor eyesight, so a small brown pickup truck can look like a male moose looking for a fight. We were in a very desolate spot when we saw the massive animal lurking behind the trees.

"Oh my gosh, there's a really BIG moose over there!" I exclaimed to Carolyn while she was driving.

"Where?" She asked as she slowed the truck.

"There, through the trees, see him? He's huge!"

"No, I can't see him," she said as she tried to keep the truck between the ditches while scanning for the giant.

"He's BIG!" I was so excited. We had seen moose on the trip, but this guy's name was Goliath I was sure. "Let's turn around, so you can see him," I suggested. She did a cop turn around and we slowly coasted by him as he was calmly eating the vegetation from the tall trees.

"Wow! He really is a big moose," Carolyn agreed when she saw him through her window. We watched him for a moment then turned the truck around again to be going in the right direction. Jesse barked and it must have startled him because suddenly, he darted through the trees keeping parallel to the road and running past the truck. We continued rolling slowly along the road, letting him get ahead of us. We were afraid that he might jump out in front of us. Well, he did. He jumped over the ditch and was about fifty feet in front of the truck when he abruptly turned and faced us straight on.

He seemed to be saying, "Bring it on, bring it on," and he started to walk towards us with a very menacing stride.

"What do we do now? What should we do?" I was frantically turning in my seat looking for an escape in the middle of nowhere. We were very nervous about this gigantic animal that was not only blocking our way, but was approaching us looking for a fight. One charge from him and my little truck would be history.

"I'm not sure, but we have to get out of here." So she whipped out another cop turn and now we were headed in the wrong direction—fast. Jesse was in the back barking up a storm at the sight of this massive animal and I was trying to tell her to be quiet, not wanting to rile Goliath any more than we already had. We traveled about half a mile around a bend then turned around again, hoping he would have left the scene. But he was still there, glaring at us from a distance. We decided that maybe if we stayed still, and far enough away so he didn't hear Jesse's constant barking, he would give up his idea that we wanted a fight. The big stare down... We won. He jumped over the ditch and headed off into the trees. Relief. We passed his spot in the road in a hurry, not really wanting to see the monster of a moose again.

That was the only scare we received from any wildlife on the trip. The scare was administered by humans, specifically, the border patrol in Prince Rupert, BC. It happened when we were departing from the ferry. OK, I hope I've been very good about not going off on big tangents like I normally do, but I simply can't avoid one here. I'll return to the border story, but have to mention the ferry trip that caused it.

We went to Skagway to visit friends from Colorado, who were living there for the summer. The plan was to visit them for a day or so before taking the Taku 2 ferry up to Haines, then down through the Inside Passage. When we went to register for the ferry, we incidentally parked next to a truck that had Colorado plates, but we didn't think much of it—Colorado is a big state. As I was getting out of the truck, a guy walked by and it was my buddy Troy! I was so shocked that I couldn't even come up with his name, stuttering at him like an idiot, "Ttttt...Ttttt...oh my gosh! What are you doing here?"

"Patti! Hey! What are you doing here?" He smiled as we hugged each and rocked back and forth with joy.

"We're getting on the ferry in a few hours."

"Really? Me too. I'm going to meet Denise in Haines."

"Cool. Hey, let's go for a beer." I introduced Troy to Carolyn (I was able to remember his name, when the shock wore off), and after doing the paperwork, we headed for a brewski before boarding the ferry together.

Troy and I had worked at Silverheels restaurant in Silverthorne that season together, and one night while we were standing in the bus station, I asked him, "What are you doing for the off season?"

"Denise and I are going to Alaska for the summer."

"Really? I'm going to Alaska too, but only for a six week trip."

"Right on."

That was all we said. No asking where either of us would be or anything. So when we bumped into each in Skagway, it was a complete surprise. Yes indeed this world can be a small place.

The ferry wasn't small though. It was an upper middle-of-the-line-sized ferry, and was plenty big enough for us. Jesse had to stay inside the truck for the journey, but I was able to take her out when we frequently stopped at the various ports. She wasn't too happy about walking over the metal grates on the bridges, but her bladder pressure convinced her that it was worth it. After the first couple of stops, she howled very loudly as if she was being tortured when I walked away from her and the truck, but she quickly settled into the routine of the breaks. She had a comfortable bed and plenty of food and water so there wasn't any reason for her to be mad. Well, except for the fun she was missing.

We met two guys who had worked for Dick Clark for years but had quit their jobs to travel throughout the forty-nine states in a van and go to baseball games in every state. Tom and Jeff were quite entertaining and full of amusing stories about life in LA and working for Dick, whom they said was a great guy. Sometimes the four of us walked around on solid ground stretching our legs and playing with Jesse during the breaks. They liked poor ol' confined-to-the-dungeon Jesse and felt bad for her.

Seeing as we had so much fun with Tom and Jeff on the ferry, they came to visit us in September and spent a few days enjoying the mountains. One day we discussed the subject of Jesse's flatulence (I would say farting, but Mum used to yell at me when I'd say that and this book is for her too). I told them that I had asked the vet about it and he said when you live at a high altitude, you definitely have more gas. Unfortunately, Jesse didn't need help in that department, she was especially, well, you know—but it didn't bother her a bit. She'd let 'em rip and not even look around to see where the noise was coming from, which is something I've seen some dogs do. It sometimes made the rest of us leave the room or it gave her a ticket to the great outdoors, but it made it easy to engage the "animal blame" answer that appears on the farter's excuse card. Jesse and her gas could be a whole chapter, but it might be offensive so I'll skip it. Anyway, Jeff and Tom had a fine visit and we still keep in touch.

OK, this tangent's over, back to leaving the ferry.

We forgot it was a border crossing as we were leaving the cargo and automobile hold on the ferry, and I was mistakenly at the wheel. Realizing it was the border, Carolyn jumped out of the truck to get Jesse's papers from the back before I could stop her. Shoot. You are not allowed to leave your vehicle when in line for a border crossing. That, paired with my nervousness at being drilled with questions, led to a search. We didn't have anything to hide, I was just nervous that they would want to see proof of citizenship, which I didn't have. The three of us sat calmly on the curb basking in the shade while they searched the whole truck for things that weren't there, and when they realized this, they let us go free. We headed out to spend time in Prince Rupert, then on to the beautiful Queen Charlotte Islands. We spent a fun filled week there with my aunt and uncle before traveling south through the heart of British Columbia to visit another aunt and uncle, and on to Vancouver to see some cousins.

At one point, we stopped to go horseback riding and had to lock Jesse in a stall. Since she had tried to follow a plane, I didn't want to take the chance that she'd try to follow the horses, which could land her in a bigger heap of trouble. She wasn't too thrilled about her confinement, but it was more spa-

191

cious than the truck and I'm sure the variety of smells kept her nose busy.

The remainder of our Alaska trip was uneventful as far as Jesse was concerned, except when she ate the whole brick of cheese. But I won't talk about that; it wasn't pretty. We returned to Summit County on June 15th just in time to enjoy a summer filled with hikes, bikes and a new kitty.

Chapter 31

Earlier in the year, Gato had been hit by a car; leaving behind a very lonely Bandit. Carolyn wanted to wait until we returned from Alaska to find another one, and she came home one afternoon with the tiny gray, black and white ball of fur. We thought the two small dots in that area were indicators that it was a he, so we named him Smithers after the town in British Columbia that we had enjoyed. We found out later that indeed the dots were freckles. Whoops. But Smithers didn't mind the masculine name—she grew into it and became more like a tomcat with all her ramblings around the neighborhood. When she first joined our family, she liked Bandit, but she certainly was wary of the large white creature who was so interested in her. She'd run and hide under the furniture or if she couldn't get there quickly enough, she'd take a swipe at Jesse's nose while emitting a vicious kitty hiss that Jesse smiled at.

But it took only about a week for little Smithers to realize that Jesse wasn't going to hurt her—she only wanted to play with her. The two formed a friendship that lasted for years. Sometimes when Jesse was lying around in the living room,

Smithers would either curl up against her and sleep, or she'd play with Jesse's tail. She'd bat the long white feathers of fur around like a tetherball, or else she'd hop onto Jesse's wagging tail and cling to it like a sailor up a mast in a hurricane, while sporting a mixed expression of panic and mischief on her cute little kitty face.

Because the two friends spent so much time together, Jesse adopted a feline habit. She learned to clean her face with her paws after a meal, and she did this frequently. She'd slowly lick her front paw and rub it back and forth over her face removing imaginary morsels of food. Since she ate every single meal of her life lying down, she was conveniently close to her paws after eating and easily washed her face. But for some reason, she stopped in mid-stroke if I looked at her. Maybe being embarrassed that she was acting like a cat or maybe just modest and didn't want to be observed washing, who knows. Sometimes I'd catch Smithers slowly licking Jesse's face and times, Jesse gave Smithers an all out bath with her huge tongue. They were great pals.

The two played together running around the apartment while Bandit sat and watched. Smithers and Bandit spent time together too, but their relationship was definitely fickle. They'd sit together and groom each , then suddenly they'd break out in a cat fight, biting and batting each , and rolling in a mass of tangled kitty fur, while Jesse watched—puzzled at this strange relationship.

I'm not sure if the three ever played together, but wonder what was going on when I came home once to find the bowl that had contained yogurt-covered peanuts on the floor, while the white dots of taste bud pleasures were scattered all over the coffee table. All three animals were crouched in the living room staring at me as if I had interrupted a game of marbles or something. Either Jesse didn't like the peanuts (doubt it) or they had just started their match, because I know that otherwise the playing pieces would have been in Jesse's stomach.

Jesse's stomach had strange tastes. I always wanted to have a contest between a loaf of bread and a juicy T-bone steak. I would have put each one on the floor, about ten feet away from her, and watched to see which one she went to first. I'll never know what she would have done, but I'd have put money on the 'ol Sunbeam bakery. She always managed to steal bread from the counter no matter how far back it was in the corner. I had to train any roommates I had, to put the bread on top of the fridge or it will be gone. I gave up on training Jesse.

Carolyn loved to have dinner parties and one day I came home to find that the freshly baked French loaves that she had for the night's gala event had been consumed by my thieving dog. Both loaves were gone without a crumb of evidence, but there wasn't a shred of doubt about the whereabouts of the bread. Jesse looked like the Goodyear Blimp. Carolyn was not happy with her and since the bakery was closed by now, I ended up going to the regular store for inferior bread and Carolyn wasn't too pleased, which was understandable.

"Where are the bagels? Did you see the loaf of bread I had yesterday? Where are the hamburger buns?" These were frequent questions I heard during my time with Jesse. I never heard "Did you see that steak I had here?" or "Where are the hot dogs?" It was always the buns. She just LOVED bread and could not stop herself from stealing it whenever someone, including myself forgot to put it out of her long pawed reach. You would think that seeing the plastic wrap on the floor, and Jesse hiding behind the table would clue me in to the fact that something was amiss, but sometimes, I just didn't notice.

I came home from church one Sunday, picked up the clear plastic bag from the floor in the living room and threw it away, not thinking a thing about it. My roommate at the time, Mary Kathryn, came in the door a few minutes later, walked into the kitchen and hollered, "Jesse!"

"What's wrong?" I walked into the kitchen.

"The bagels."

"What bagels?"

"The bag of four specialty bagels I bought this morning."

"I didn't see any bagels this morning."

"I know. I bought them while you were at church. I came home, put them on the counter, but had to go out for a minute, and now they're gone!"

"Oh, that's what the wrapper on the floor was, oops. I'll go and get some more."

"You can't. The bakery closes at noon on Sunday. Shoot, Jesse."

Jesse ruined many a meal by stealing the bread item. One time I was at my mom's house with my brother Dave, and we were settling in to an outdoor supper of yummy grilled hot dogs, when my mom asked, "Patti, please get the buns."

"Where are they?"

"On the ledge by the side door."

I walked to the door, didn't see the buns and walked back. "Are you sure you put them there?"

"Yes."

I walked back to check again when I noticed the plastic wrap lying on the ground. "Jesse!" I strolled into the back yard with the empty bun bag and saw Jesse hiding behind the table. "Well. Jesse ate them."

"The whole bag? No." Dave was shocked.

"Yup, the whole bag."

"How'd she get them? They were up on the ledge?"

"She's a breadaholic, Dave. She always finds a way." I wasn't surprised at her athletic ability at all and we ate bun-less dogs that night.

I've always wondered what dogs are thinking when they're sleeping and their legs are wiggling, jiggling and running to nowhere. People say that they're chasing rabbits or some kind of animal, but in Jesse's case, it was the bread truck. I'm sure of it.

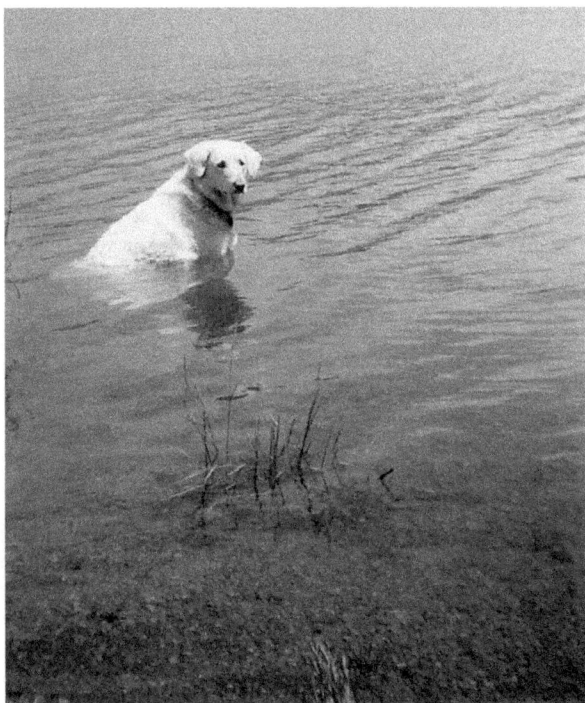

Water can be a life saver too.

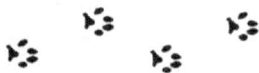

Chapter 32

I'm not sure why people think that waiters and waitresses are weathermen, entertainment guides and city maps, but they do. Guess it's because we worked in a resort area. We were asked all sorts of silly questions, like, why didn't we get the snow they predicted, or why are we getting the snow they didn't predict, or is it still downhill to ride from Copper Mountain resort (elevation 9600 feet) to Frisco (elevation 9097 feet)? No. They raised the town 500 feet. What do you think? I was sitting out on the patio one semi-cloudy afternoon at Charity's restaurant where Carolyn worked, when a lady actually asked Carolyn, "When is it going to stop raining?"

Carolyn looked up at the sky and answered, "I guess when that cloud goes by." She wasn't meaning to be rude, but what a silly question. One man even asked her how in the world do you get the stew inside the hollowed out bread loaf. "With a ladle." I have even heard the question, "At what elevation do the deer turn into elk?" Either that lady definitely left her brain at home when she started on vacation, or she sped through the tunnel. Who knows? We, up here in Summit County, have come to realize that visitors are just so darn excited to be up here in the beautiful Rocky Mountains, that they travel through the long Eisenhower Tunnel so fast, it just sucks their brains right out. It's a joke, but sometimes we wonder...

One waitress I worked with once said that she was going to write a book about all the silly and stupid things that people say and do in a restaurant and call it, "The Fat Man Always Sits in the Aisle". I thought it was funny because it's kinda true.

Yes, I have been asked some doozies but, "How did you get that shiner?" was a legitimate question. As you know, Jesse was a night dog and we often played, or went for walks when I returned home from work. Well, one night we were playing ball in the house, which was rare. Actually, it was rare for us to be playing with a ball anyplace. Remember, she wasn't a typical retriever. So anyway, I was crawling around on my hands and knees, getting the ball and wrestling with Jesse, when she slid to get the ball from the corner, whirled around and charged into me with her rock hard retriever head, hitting me in the right eye and slamming me to the floor. I hollered, rolled over and lay there for a moment. That hurt! I stood up and looked in the mirror just in time to see a "Good and Plenty" candy shaped bump magically appear underneath my eye. It was like a great special effects moment from a movie. Even Spielberg would have been proud. Game over. I had to put ice on my sore face.

My mom called early the next morning and when I answered the phone next to my bed, I realized that my eye could barely see over my cheek that was in the way. I told her, "I think Jesse gave me a black eye last night."

And indeed she did. A really good one. It turned the right side of my face black, blue and purple and I had some people tell me it was the best shiner they'd ever seen. One group of six men that I waited on a few nights later, wanted to "get the guy who did that to me" and when I told them it was my dog, they listened to the story and had a good laugh. They believed me and we had a great time. That night, two guys agreed that retrievers have the hardest heads in the dog world and they even gave me a big tip. It was interesting to me that when the eye was deep black and fresh, and I told people the story, everyone believed me. But why would I make that up? Funny how I received fantastic sympathy tips.

But when the colors had turned to yellow, green and light brown it was a whole different story. One Friday night, I was lucky to get any tips at all. I had a cold with a slight sniff, was sporting my colorful healing eye, and told customers (who asked about it) that my dog ran into me. I honestly think people thought I was a semi-creative lying drug addict, with a boyfriend who beat me, and I got the worse tips of my life. It almost became funny because it was so consistent. I wanted to lean down to a table of people who gave me a five percent tip and ask them, "What the heck are you thinking?" But I knew what they were thinking; their faces said it all.

I really enjoyed my job at Silverheels Southwestern Grill restaurant. The people I worked with were wonderful and most of the customers were great, so we had a lot of fun there. Another reason was because we closed down for a while in the slow seasons, so it allowed me time to travel.

Jesse accompanied me on any driving trips and was always excited to see that big red suitcase come out of the closet.

Chicago or Canada to see family, Nashville to see friends, or just plain traveling, we did it all. Truckers were funny to listen to on the CB—talking about the big white bear that sat next to the girl in the pick up truck. Friends used to tell me that I should travel with a gun for protection, but Jesse was all I needed and I felt safe. Besides, I always knew that the good Lord was watching over us and we were never alone.

I know there are people who don't like people's dogs to come and visit them, but I never had that problem with Jesse. Of course family and friends are usually tolerant, but because Jesse ended up being a well-mannered dog, we went everywhere and Jesse made friends all over the country. (I should say; she was well mannered towards others but she still didn't *always* listen to me when I asked her to do things.)

Whenever we stopped for gas, after she stretched her legs, she'd always sit outside the store and wait for me, greeting the customers as they went by. She could have been the 7-11 poster dog, and she got away with being allowed inside the stores many times when it was cold. I don't know why people felt sorry for her—she had a beautiful thick coat. But she'd just look at them and smile, they'd oblige her, and in the door she'd go. She'd sit on the inside by the door and wait for me to pay, and then we'd be on our way.

Antiques are my favorite type of furniture and since prices are much better in the South and East, than in the West, we always stopped in certain towns to shop for treasures. We were in Chillicothe, Missouri when I saw a marvelous mission rocker that I had to have. It was in a store where I stopped to browse and had spent time talking and laughing with the owner. But disappointment set in, when he told me he didn't take Visa. I thought it was everywhere I wanted to be. Since I was heading home, had spent almost all of my cash, and the banks were closed, I was out of luck.

He saw my disappointment and said, "Well, I might be crazy, but you can take the rocker and mail a check to me."

"Really?" What a nice guy. I told him I'd call someone to let them know what was going on, so if anything happened to me, they could mail him the money for his rocking chair. As he carried my rocker and we stepped through the doorway, right by my truck, I pointed and told him, "This is my truck."

He looked up and saw Jesse sitting in the cab, smiling at him through the window and he said, "Is that your dog?"

"Yeah, that's Jesse."

"Well anyone who has a dog with a face like that, I know I can trust."

Tickled by his comment and a little curious about the basis of trust (he must have been a dog lover), I told him, yes he could trust me and I mailed him the money as soon as I returned home to rock the summer away in my new ancient chair.

During another summer when we were returning to Colorado and back to work, there was a record heat wave. Since I like to make the trip in one day and prefer traveling in daylight, we were stuck traveling with a thousand people on the third of July through the middle of Nebraska during this incredible heat. It was so hot that the air conditioner couldn't even run as my poor truck would overheat even faster. Everyone on the road had to stop at all the rest stops to cool their engines and their bodies, so there was a sense of miserable camaraderie. The sprinklers were on at every stop and children were running around splashing and playing, while the adults were refilling radiators with water, and trying to take advantage of any shade available. It would have been a grand social affair if we weren't so worried our vehicles would blow up, or the children and dogs would keel over in the heat.

It was the closest I came to losing Jesse. She was sitting inside with me because I wanted to keep an eye on her and at one point, I saw that her tongue was hanging out longer than ever before, she was panting with high speed breaths and her eyes started to glaze over. I told her to hang on and hurried to the next exit to wet her down at a gas station. It helped for a while, but back on the road, soon she was glassy eyed again. I had asked if there were any lakes in the vicinity, because if I could get her in cool water, it would help. There was one about forty five miles away.

We stopped again and again, but the heat was like an ocean wave chasing us and we couldn't get away. Wetting Jesse down wasn't the answer. So I raced down the highway on the lookout for cops, but was more concerned that Jesse was fading from heat stroke. Never in my life have I been so happy to see the sign for Grand Island. I whipped the truck into the state park and hurried into the water, with Jesse at my side. We sat in the cool refreshing water for almost an hour and I was grateful when her eyes lost the glassy look, her panting slowed, and her tongue rolled back up into her mouth. When I was pruned, wrinkly, and cool, I got out and sat on the bank of the life-saving lake while Jesse stayed in the water. It had been a close call.

That was about the worst event that happened to us on our travels. Even when there was truck trouble, we usually lucked out and were never stranded.

One night as we were heading home to Colorado, my fuel pump started failing. We were in the vicinity of the small farm town of Adair, Iowa. I pulled off the highway to learn that everything was closed, so I got back on the entrance ramp so we could roll to a start in the morning. A trucker stopped to help me figure out the problem. He stayed in his truck on the entrance ramp with us, and the next morning, he followed us to the exit ramp for Adair; making sure everything was OK. I was very grateful to him. He told me he had a sister and hoped that someone would do the same for her. He was a good man.

Lucky for me, the guy at the garage was able to locate the fuel pump despite it being a holiday weekend, and Jesse and I spent the better part of yet another traveling July third, visiting with the elderly owners of the garage. They liked Jesse and let her sprawl out by the fan to keep cool. We eventually were back on the road and made it home safely in time for fireworks on the fourth. I stopped to visit with those folks years later to see how they were doing. They didn't remember me right away, but suddenly, the old fellow said, "Oh, you're the one with the big white dog, from Colorado." Yup, people always remembered Jesse.

Chapter 33

Jesse had a beautiful and expressive face around those intelligent and forever-alert retriever eyes. She smiled a lot and talked to me through her eyes that never missed a thing. Anyone who loves and is around animals a lot would probably agree that they do seem to talk to you at times. They look at you intensely in answer to questions, comments and ordinary conversation. I also think they can have a rather extensive vocabulary—contrary to the Far Side comic and Frasier episode that claim all they know is their name, and the rest is "blah, blah, blah..." Jesse even learned to spell t-r-e-a-t, so I even had to lip sync that word.

She was smart but also generally a happy-go-lucky dog, sometimes mischievous and still strong-headed, but every now and then she was afraid of something. For some reason, ever since we moved to Colorado, there was something in the air that scared her. In Denver, sometimes she'd sit outside and bark at seemingly nothing—with a scared look on her face, and when we moved up to the mountains, it was worse. She used to bark at nothing and then she'd suddenly take off trotting around the yard, doing laps around the entire building with her

Patricia A. White

tail tucked, her ears pinned back and a frightened look on her face. I never figured out why she did this, but I have a feeling it had to do with elk.

Whenever elk meat was being cooked, as soon as the aroma of the elk filled the air, Jesse would start trotting around the apartment with that scared look on her face. I used to try to catch her, to try to hold her still and pet her, but she wouldn't let me. She always issued a slow, low, deep woof that came from the bottom of her throat—all while doing the laps.

And she did it in places than our house, so I knew it wasn't our stove or oven that sent her off running.

When my brother Dave was living in Summit County for a season, one spring day Jesse and I went over to his house for a barbecue. It was that great time of year when you're knee deep in snow with shorts and a tank top on, or no shirt at all if you're a guy. The three of us were on the deck when Dave put the cool meat on the hot grill. It sizzled and suddenly Jesse jumped up, put her nose in the air and took off running around the yard, and then disappeared behind the corner of the house.

"Where in the world did she go?" Dave asked with a puzzled expression.

"Well, I'm not sure, but, is that elk?" I asked as I pointed to the grill.

"Yeah. Why?"

"Thought so. That explains it."

Jesse appeared at the corner of the house and trotted through the snow to circle the house again, with her tail tucked, ears pinned and *that* face. Dave watched with the spatula in one hand, beer in the and a totally confused look on his face.

"Explains what?"

"I'm not sure exactly. She does this whenever she smells elk meat cooking. Bizarre isn't it?"

208

"Ah, yeah."

"She'll settle down when it's done cooking," I casually assured him. Jesse eventually quit doing laps and we had a tasty lunch in the warm Colorado sun.

But it wasn't only the scent of elk meat cooking that sent her running. One year my sister sent me some lamb's wool slippers for Christmas. I brought the package into the kitchen, excitedly opened the box and pulled out the wonderful slippers. Immediately, Jesse stood up, sniffed them and took off running around the apartment in a panic. I set the slippers in the box on the floor but Jesse hid in my bedroom. I was curious if it really was the slippers, so I took them into the bedroom, and Jesse bolted out; nearly knocking me over. "What a weirdo," I thought to myself. She was eventually able to be in the same room with the slippers as long as they were on my feet, but I never did figure out her strange behavior.

And it was strange when she refused food of any kind. Once when I was at my mom's, we were sitting downstairs to eat while watching TV, which is something we didn't do often —unless there was a hockey game on. We had take-out from the local stand that specializes in gyros. Eagerly taking my first big bite of the taco that was overflowing with crisp lettuce, sharp cheddar cheese, fresh onions and ripe tomatoes and yuk... the meat was lamb. I don't eat lamb. My taste buds reject it. Oh well, there goes my supper to the dogs. I set the taco on the floor and Jesse came over. One sniff and she took off trotting around the family room in her usual tucked up position, woofing deeply.

"What the heck is Jesse doing?" my mom asked as she stared at my wacko dog.

"She's scared."

"What's she scared of, it's a taco."

"I know. She does this crazy thing when she's smells elk cooking and sees or smells lamb slippers. She panics. Look at her face," I casually commented as I melted into the couch in hungry disappointment. "I knew she didn't like my lamb slippers, but I thought she might eat the meat. I've never known her to refuse food. Weird, huh."

So my mom's dog enjoyed my taco while Jesse ran around the house looking for elk.

Dogs bark. Usually they have a reason, so we don't mind. But when they sit and bark for no reason that we can see or hear, it's annoying. I think it was because of the elk... why Jesse became one of those barking dogs while she lived in Colorado. I finally was tired of listening to her, so I decided to try to train her not to bark. I used a bit of psychology on her. Whether it was Operant or Classical Conditioning, I can't remember. I always got the mice in the maze confused with Pavlov's Dogs.

"No barking, Jesse, and I'll give you a treat. OK?" I told her as I let her out.

"But I might have to bark."

"No you don't. There is nothing out there and you know it."

"But..."

"No barking."

I'd let her back inside after a few minutes of not barking. "Good girl, Jesse. You didn't bark," and I gave her a treat for a reward. The next time she wanted to go out, I'd let her out and tell her, "No barking, Jesse, and I'll give you a treat, OK?"

"O-kaaay. I'll try Mom."

"Try hard, Jesse." She'd be out for a little longer, without barking, so she'd get a treat. We repeated this pattern and soon, she was going outside for a long time without barking and the neighbors were happy again.

But it didn't take her long to realize that by going out and not barking, she was getting her favorite treats. And it didn't dawn on me that she figured this out until one day she went back and forth a million times.

"Mom, I have to go out."

"OK, Jesse." I let her out. Five minutes later, she was knocking at the glass door.

"Mom, I want to come in."

"OK Jesse." I let her in and after her treat, she sat in the living room.

Five minutes later, she was up at the door, "Mom, I have to go out."

"OK Jesse." I let her out. Five minutes later, she was knocking at the glass door.

"Mom I want to come in."

"OK Jesse." I let her in and after her treat, she sat in the living room.

Five minutes later, she was up at the door, "Mom, I have to go out."

"Jesse, you were just out."

"I know, but I have to go out."

"OK, Jesse." I let her out and watched what she did, thinking that she had diarrhea or was sick. She wasn't. She sat there and smiled at me. I returned to my seat, only to be interrupted shortly by her knock. I let her in, and while reaching for the box of treats, I heard her snicker and suddenly knew what she was doing. The tables were turned. She was the trainer and I was the trainee... and she had done a good job of it too.

Chapter 34

Living in Colorado and continuing to work at Silverheels meant keeping busy at work in the winter and summer seasons and traveling during parts of the spring and fall, and it was during the summer of 1990 that one of my lifelong dreams came true. I was lucky enough to buy a beautiful black four year old gelding named Ringo. He was a terrific horse. He was very even tempered, smart, and a joy to ride. He belonged to a friend of mine and I had ridden and even camped with him the summer before, but now he was my new friend to take care of and enjoy. Jesse was able to go with us on many excursions in the mountains and the two were pals of sorts. I was completely happy with my wonderful life and all was going along swell... then I fell in love.

I met him one night when my friend Dave and I had been riding and went to eat at a local bar and grill. I fell in very fast and very deep, but I must say that it was different than what happened with Danny nine years later.

Martin had a young black chow mix dog named Nanook, whom Jesse liked right away. They played constantly, running around in the snow and chasing each over snow banks, crashing together and then doing it all over again and again. It was great to see Jesse running around like a youngster.

Martin wanted to move back to Allentown, Pennsylvania. I loved him, wanted to be with him, and decided to go. Even though there was an odd feeling deep inside me on the day we left, I was committed to the move. I knew the road went both ways and I would always wonder what would have happened if I didn't go. So I went—thinking everything would be fine. Perhaps we'd get married, stay there, and I'd be living closer to my family; especially the Canadian gang.

We moved to the hamlet named Richlandtown, which was a quiet little spot nestled between rolling farmland and forests, forty miles north of Philadelphia. We found a wonderful place with fifty acres, two bass ponds and all sorts of beautiful trees. Jesse and Nanook had loads of room in which to run and play, and could go swimming wherever they wanted. I was fortunate to find a place to keep Ringo just five minutes away and there were plenty of places where I could ride. Many times, Jesse, Ringo and I went to the large lake nearby and had fun outings enjoying the smell of leaves on the ground and the amazing colors that the east has to offer in the fall. So everything was great... except the relationship.

I started to work in the insurance business with The Franklin Life Insurance Company and when an invitation came to go to the head office in Springfield Illinois, I wasn't sure if I should go. My mind was abruptly made up when my brother called to tell me that our mom had cancer. So I went to Illinois to see my mom just after her surgery and surprised everyone with a short visit, while Jesse stayed in Pennsylvania. When my mom discovered that things weren't going well for me, she suggested that I move home for a while to sort things out.

An explanation about the whole relationship and my beliefs about it could be included, but it won't. Suffice it to say that I made a big mistake, or had a big learning curve experience as I'd like to think of it. God knows why we take certain paths and unfortunately we usually don't see why until we look back and hopefully say, "Oh yeah, that's why that happened". At least I realized my misstep and did something about it.

I returned to Pennsylvania by train, and was fortunate enough to enjoy the incredible Horseshoe Curve in the Allegheny Mountains outside of Altoona; while the trees were wearing their brilliant fall colors—absolutely spectacular! Two weeks after returning, I loaded up my belongings, Ringo and Jesse, and I headed home to Illinois.

It was a hard period in my life, but looking back, there were some good things that happened. My relationship with my family was strengthened—especially with my mom—and I learned things about myself that I wouldn't have, if I hadn't been through this turmoil. I was able to be there for my mom during her recovery from cancer and she was able to be there for me during my recovery from stupidity. I became a more assertive person, made some new friends in Illinois and spent time with some of my old ones. I don't regret the whole experience and I hope I know better for the next one. I think it's true that what doesn't kill you makes you stronger, and, it's OK to use the future to be happy today, but don't be happy only in the future. In words, don't think, "I'll be happy when...", but think, "Yes, things will get better in time." And they always do.

At the time, my mom had a dog named Tressie, who was a show quality Sheltie. She and Jesse became great friends during the months we lived there. They'd hang out together in the yard sharing life stories or just lying around. It always made me laugh, when they were both standing at the door and for some reason I wanted one of them to stay in. "Jesse you stay, Tressie you go out. No Jesse, you stay. Go on Tressie, you go out. No Jess, stay. Go Tress, go." Abbott and Costello's routine, "Who's On First?" always popped into my head as they'd look at me shouting, "Make up your mind!" I wanted to rename one of them Spot, just to make it easier for all of us.

Ringo lived at my sister's small farm, and Jesse and I went out there every week for a visit. I'd call Ringo and give him grain on the ground in the pasture if I didn't have time to go for a ride. One time, Jesse was lying down eating the grain when Ringo thundered up to us and lowered his head to eat it. Jesse actually growled at him as if it was her meal he was sharing. I couldn't believe the nerve she had, and told her she'd better get up and let him eat his grain in peace before he made a rug out of her.

Jesse loved the farm. She played with their dogs and cats, and chased after any wild rabbits that happened to be around. One day, however, my niece's bunny Ramada was accidentally let out, and Jesse and Friskie (their dog) treated her like a wild bunny; no more Ramada. We felt really bad, but it's hard to take the hunter instinct out of dogs, especially if they've eaten rabbits before.

One day we went to look at pot-bellied pigs, and saw a whole barnyard full of all kinds of animals that shouldn't get along. The Dr. Doolittle of that place was a laid-back old fellow who said that they just all get along, and the dogs knew to leave the bunnies alone. Jesse wouldn't fit in; she loved to eat rabbits far more than she liked to listen to anyone.

And she still wasn't listening to me all the time when I told her to stay in the truck. One day, I took her with me to shop for shoes and run some errands. I was feeling bad that we hadn't been out getting exercise or spending much time together, because I was working over eighty hours a week (to pay off the debt I had incurred during my stupidity concerning Martin), so off we went to tour the suburban stores of Chicago. I pulled into the Chernan's shoe store parking lot and told Jesse to stay in the truck. She was a good girl in her older age so it had been a long time since I'd heard it, but while I was shoe shopping, there it was. That familiar announcement came over the intercom. "Attention shoppers, we have a large white dog in the store. Would the owner please come and get their dog."

Jesse! I hurried along the racks of shoes, just in time to see her tail go flying by. A manager came running up the row of racks and yelled, "It went that way."

People were running all over the place after her—leaving shoe boxes scattered everywhere. I really didn't know why everyone was in such a panic. The commotion was almost bizarre! It's not like she was attacking anyone, and they weren't serving food or anything—it was a shoe store. But I found out that the idea of having a dog in the store was not nearly as accepted as it had been in the South, or as admired as it was in the resort towns of Colorado where there were dogs hanging out in almost every store.

But I really can't fault those novice suburbanites for panicking. They didn't know she was a seasoned shopper. She had been welcome in many stores, but I guess shoe stores were out of the running. I'm not saying that it was fine for her to be in there, but things sure were stirred up quickly. People caught her by the front door and when I ran up there, a sweet lady kindly said, "Oh she's scared and was looking for you."

"Thanks for holding her," I smiled at the lady as I bent to pet Jesse and comfort her.

I'll say she was scared at that point. Everyone was chasing her, she couldn't find me and I couldn't find her. I shuffled her out to the truck, and because I was so embarrassed, I left.

I went to my favorite Chicago Hot Dog place, parked, and sternly and I mean sternly, told Jesse to STAY in the truck this time. While I was in line, one of the three women who were sitting by the window near the truck commented, "Look at that dog. What a pretty dog."

"Look how good she is, sitting there in the truck." said another.

"She just stays in the truck, what a well behaved dog."

"Is that your dog?" one of them asked me, noticing that I was constantly watching her.

"Yes she is."

"Well, what a good dog, just sitting there."

"She had better just sit there if she knows what's good for her," I fumed.

"Doesn't she always stay there?"

"Nope, and she just came from shoe shopping at Chernens."

"You mean she went into the store?"

"She sure did, and I'm mad at her. I didn't get to buy my shoes. She's in trouble and she knows it."

"Oh."

They didn't know what else to say because they sensed my mood so they turned their attention back to their food. I just couldn't let them think Jesse was a great and wonderful dog. I was too mad at her. I hate shopping and now because of her antics, I'd have to go shoe shopping another time. Alone.

Time passed by, and I enjoyed living in Illinois with my family, but my wounds were healing. It was the spring of 1992 and I was thinking it was soon time to go back to Colorado. It was where I belonged. My heart was there and I needed to rejoin it.

An Irish Pub

Chapter 35

Rejoining or following your heart. Yeah sure it's a great idea, but unfortunately, for many of us this is not usually possible. Life gets in the way of doing those crazy or maybe not so crazy things we want to do. Taking a class for a trade or an art that we like. Taking a long trip. Quitting a job we hate, and doing something we like instead, even if it is for less pay. Whatever. You know. But, unlike the Nike ad, we just don't do it. Maybe we don't follow our heart because we're not exactly sure what our heart is saying to us. In this time of faster faster more more be successful and thrive, how do we take the time to really listen to what our hearts are saying? And sometimes, listening can be frustrating if we have a heart that knows what it wants, but it wants too many different things. Be here, be there, be everywhere.

Go to any bookstore and you'll find plenty of self-help books that can at least try to lead us in the right direction when following our hearts. "Simple Abundance" by Sarah Ban Breathnach is a great day book. It's teaching me to get to know myself better and be in touch with some of the signals that get flashed across the highways and byways of my being. It's a great help, but I have yet to read the whole book because I travel in the spring and fall, and heavy self help books aren't my idea of vacation reading. But maybe they should be.

When I returned from that trip to Ireland and Scotland in the fall of 2000, I was miserable. I wanted to be back in Ireland. It was where my heart had stayed. I wasn't ready to start a new life in another mountain range of Colorado at the start of winter—even though that had been my plan. My mind kept seeing Greenane; the mystic castle, the shore walk, the farms, the pubs and of course, Danny.

I visited with many of my friends, telling the stories about Ireland and how everything happened with Danny and being able to see him time and time again. It amazed me how fate had repeatedly stepped in and allowed me to see him. I told my friends that I really wanted to go back to Ireland. I was thinking it'd be the perfect time to go and write my book about Jesse that I had wanted to write for over seven years.

All of my friends said I should go. Why not? It was the perfect time. When would I get the chance again? My belongings were in storage, my horse Jimmy (whom I bought 3 years earlier) was in great hands, and if I could afford it, go for it. But I wasn't sure it was the sane thing to do.

So I floated around the county in a fog, trying to do the things that were necessary for moving, but I couldn't get Greenane and Danny out of my mind. One day I went to the post office to pick up a moving kit. When I took it out of the rack and looked at it, I heaved a heavy sigh. I had been making a real effort not to think about Danny, and this packet had a photo on the front of it of a little boy carrying a box on his head. And do you know what the box said? Danny's things. Not Billy's, Bobby's, or Tommy's, but Danny's. OK. That's OK. Just a coincidence. So I headed to Wal-Mart to pick up the photos from the trip, and when I walked in, there was a huge square display of cartons of apples for sale. Now, I have never known our Wal-Mart to sell apples, and later when I asked friends about the mysterious apple sale, they hadn't ever seen them in Wally World either. Do you know what brand of apples they were? Danny Boy Apples!

All right, that's OK, I said to myself, just another coincidence—albeit a strange one. So I picked up my eleven packages of photos and randomly opened one to see how they turned out and what do you think the first photos were? Nope, not Danny—those were developed in Galway, Ireland. It was Greenane. Of all the photos of all the places in Ireland and Scotland that I could have opened, Greenane was first. "What is going on here? Is someone trying to tell me something?" I was just plain confused now. Being one of those people who believe in signs from above, I was questioning these very questionable signs.

I didn't know what to do because I felt in my heart that I should be back in Greenane but that was crazy. I called Sean one day, telling him that I wanted to be there, and he said, "Oh for fect's sake, get on a plane and come back then."

That didn't help my dilemma. Wasn't I supposed to be finding a new place to live, finding a new job and "getting on with my life"?

While visiting with my friend Karen at her house that overlooked the stunning Ten Mile and Gore Range Mountains, I sat admiring the scene I'd seen so many times over the years and was telling her about the trip and my current feelings. At one point, without even thinking, I said, "If I don't go back, I'll regret it for the rest of my life." It just popped out. My word controller was broken—again. I was shocked to say the least and asked Karen, "Did I just say that?" as tears started to slowly stream down my cheeks.

"Yes, you did Patti." Karen slowly and thoughtfully answered.

In that instant, I knew I was going back. I had to. No more decision making. Now it was just a matter getting everything ready to go back to Ireland to write my book. Whether it was feasible financially or not, I couldn't stand to have that big regret hanging over my head for the rest of my life. It has been said: "I'd rather regret something I did, than something I didn't do." I knew I might never get the chance again.

Preparations commenced for the trip. I moved the rest of my household belongings and my motorcycle to my storage space in Cedaredge; the town where Jimmy was living. I easily found the notes I had been compiling over the years for the book. I checked my bank accounts and deposited enough money for the three months I'd be living in Ireland. Then I called Sean.

"Hi Sean, How's it going?"

"Grand, Patti. Are ya well?"

"Yeah, I am. I guess."

"Good."

"Well Sean, I've decided. I'm coming back. I'm going to write the book about my dog Jesse that I've wanted to write for years."

"Oh ya are, are ya?"

"Yup. Is there any way we can work out an arrangement for longer term board?"

"Aye, sure, no problem. When are ya comin'?"

"In about 2 weeks. I have some things to organize before I leave."

"Oh that's grand. Just let me know."

"Sean... do you think I'm crazy?"

"Aye. But ya might as well come 'n do it. There're a lot of animal lovers in the world ya know."

I was encouraged by his words but that didn't really matter. I was doing this for my mum, my sister and myself.

I needed a laptop computer and found one that suited my needs perfectly for just two hundred dollars. I called my long distance friends who knew Jesse and asked them for any anecdotes about her that they particularly liked. My old roommate Mary Kathryn, was so excited for me. "I never thought that one of my friends would ever be calling to tell me that they were going to Ireland to write a book. That's awesome Patti!"

It was crazy. I couldn't believe I was going. It seemed like something I had read in a romance novel, but at the same time, I knew I had to go back.

Because everything was falling into place so well, it was getting less nerve wracking and more exciting. I'd write my book, and either get Ireland and especially Danny, out of my system, or I'd stay there. When I called to purchase my airline ticket, I hung up the phone and said, "Yes! I'm really going." Somehow I felt good about this thing I had to do.

When famous people write books about their lives, we're in awe and sometimes envious of their exciting and adventuresome lives. I'm just an ordinary person and have enjoyed being a waitress for most of my life; hardly near the top of society's success scale. But I feel very fortunate that I was able to go and follow my heart—and try to fulfill a goal or two. You really can do anything, if you put your mind to it. I was on my way back to Ireland to write my book. It was something I had wanted to do for a long time. So I boarded a plane on November 13, 2000, to return to a very special place. A place I thought I'd never see again. You know the saying...never say never.

New friends.

Chapter 36

I didn't think it would ever get here, but it did. Time. It was time to move back to Colorado. I was emotionally and financially ready. Now, it was the summer of 1992 and I flew my friend Bob in to Chicago to help me drive back out to Denver. He stayed for a few days to see the city because he'd never been there, and we went to the "Taste of Chicago". When a tornado came extremely close to the downtown area, throwing tables and trash barrels into the turbulent green waters of Lake Michigan and scattering people like a Japanese Godzilla film while whipping dirt into any open hole in your head, he really did get a taste of Chicago.

He also had a taste of the hot sultry Midwest summer evenings when the lightning bugs rise slowly and mysteriously from the ground to light the night with their soft glow. He shouted in near panic when he saw the tiny lights in the trees, thinking we were being invaded by miniature flying aliens with teeny tiny headlamps strapped to their butts. Well, when I caught one and showed him the fluorescent bulb in the tiny body, he was amazed. It was so cool to see his reaction. It's great when you can share the wonder of a common event with someone who has never seen it. It reminds us to bring out the kid inside and enjoy the simple things all over again. It had been a long time since I had enjoyed the fluorescent green glow of a lightning bug's butt—up close and radiant.

So after a few fun filled Illinois summer days of riding horses and touring around, we loaded everything into the truck and trailer, and Jesse, Ringo, Bob and I were westward bound. Two people and a large dog in a cab for over a thousand miles is not the most comfortable way to travel. I heard a thousand times: "Jesse, move over, you're sitting on me." Poor Bob.

We arrived in Denver in the afternoon and I didn't want Ringo to stay in the trailer while I rested, so we put him in the very small backyard. He snorted at the water in the above ground pool right before Bob brought him fresh water, but he was calm and mellow—not to mention very tired from traveling, so he settled in quickly. Jesse was sitting with us in the side yard and Bob had just finished saying, "Wouldn't it be funny if the landlords showed up right now to check out our fridge?"

They did.

Seeing Jesse, they asked, "Whose dog is this? It's not yours is it Bob?"

"No, but come see our new dog," Bob said as he walked towards the fence.

"It's a horse!" She screamed. "What's a horse doing in the yard?!"

"Resting." Bob's honest answer.

Luckily they were easygoing people and when we explained why Ringo was there, they didn't really mind. They knew he'd be gone shortly, when the three of us headed to the mountains, which we did later that evening.

We ended up living with Carolyn and her roommate Jay, until we could find a spot of our own. We were a mix between "Three's Company" and "The Incredible Journey"—two cats, two dogs, two females and a guy. Jesse met Sophie and was reunited with Bandit and Smithers. Bandit sulked away—mad that there were two of them now, while Smithers was all over Jesse, purring and kissing her face.

Sophie was Carolyn's purebred golden retriever who was four months old and full of energy. Jesse loved young dogs, but now she was older and her level of patience had decreased. So when Sophie jumped on her head repeatedly, Jesse put her in her place with a quick growl, but never actually went after her. When Sophie jumped all over my head, which she did every morning while I slept on the couch, I simply put my hand down and petted her on her chest. She became like a Snoopy vulture, hypnotized, hanging her head and staring, but she was smiling.

Jesse and I ended up moving next door so now we were neighbors. It was great fun. Dinner parties, walking buddies, mountains to enjoy—life was back to normal. We went for a lot of walks, and Sophie would usually take Jesse's leash in her mouth and tug her along the street, which greatly amused Carolyn and me. A small feisty golden pup who was jumping up and down leading a nonchalant old gal who merely looked at Sophie and strolled calmly around the neighborhood was the usual scene. At least Sophie was obeying the leash law... and I suppose Jesse didn't mind because she always let Sophie do it. They were a funny pair.

During this time, whenever I had to go on a trip and couldn't take Jesse with me, Carolyn watched Jesse and she was forever putting her on a diet. She thought that topping one hundred pounds and falling in between the obese and over-weight categories on the official dog weight chart was just too much weight for Jesse. Jesse hated when I left, but admittedly, she looked slimmer and happier when I returned. She was able to keep most of the weight off of her, but when she'd lie by the food dish, put her head on the edge of the bowl and moan, it was hard to completely ignore her.

At first it was a soft moan and I could shut her out, but as the moan became louder, longer and more desperate, it was impossible to ignore her. "Oh Jesse, you're pathetic," I'd tell her shaking my head.

"But Mom, I'm hungry."

"No you're not, you just think you are."

"No, Mom. I really am hungry," as she'd moan even louder.

"Jesse, it's not supper time yet, you have to wait."

"But I'm withering away to nothing but skin and bones."

"Jesse you look great. My Jane Russell dog is gone." We always called her that because she was such a full-figured gal.

She'd look up at me with those sad retriever eyes, begging me to relieve her of the misery of the diet, and even though I knew it was reinforcing the behavior, I'd give in and give her a few morsels of food. At least it silenced the moaning.

My roommate at the time was a guy named Michael who really liked Jesse, and she liked him. He was financially set and was just taking a break from the working grind, so he had a lot of time on his hands. Jesse liked to hang out with him and sometimes he'd lie in front of the TV and use her back as a pillow and she'd just lie there and not even move. Many times he'd take her with him when he went cross-country skiing. Jill and Kiwi went along sometimes too and they'd all have a great time on the trails.

It was strange for me when she was gone and I was home alone. The house just wasn't the same. By this time Jesse and I had been together for eleven years and it was usually just the two of us. Since I'd had only two serious relationships, everywhere I went; it was me 'n Jess. When people said I could bring a friend, I'd ask, "Can I bring Jesse?" (If I thought it was an event that allowed dogs.) I even brought her to church for a Sunday afternoon service in the park and everyone loved her. Matter of fact, that's when the photo on the back cover was taken—I was trying to keep my cake and pop out of her reach.

We had traveled all over the States and many parts of Canada and we were almost always together. She had been with me through all the ups and downs of life and she was my best friend. I had shed many a tear onto her understanding white fur and had loads of laughs, many provided by Jesse herself.

But I wasn't laughing when I returned home from a hut trip and she was gone. Colorado has a fantastic system of huts in the mountains that you can ski to and spend the night. They're quite accommodating and comfortable, and usually the trips are a blast. This trip however wasn't exactly that way.

There were about 10 of us who decided to go up to the Frasier Hut to celebrate our friend Tina's birthday. So we gathered at Camp Hale, outside of Leadville, and got ready for the fun trip. After skiing along the flats, it was time to ascend. We put skins on our skis and headed up. (Skins are strips of various materials to keep you from sliding backwards.) Because my skins were so heavy, it was like strapping concrete blocks on my feet and walking up hill for four miles. Not my idea of fun on any given day. It was a shared opinion with the others who had heavy skins on their skis.

At the halfway point up the mountain, there were a few tears shed by a couple of the girls and the thought of going back down was discussed, but we pushed on. When I reached the cabin in immense pain, I was ready to throw the hated skins over the side of the mountain—never to be seen again. But they weren't mine, so I couldn't. Instead, we went inside and all had a great time celebrating Tina's birthday, even though some of us could hardly walk.

Because the pain was still around when I came home, finding out that Jesse was gone wasn't the ending to the trip I would have liked. I called Animal Control, and yes they had her (this time she had a name and address tag—something I think all dogs should have). I hurried to the shelter to get her, but they said I couldn't take her until I had the ticket from the police. Why they didn't tell me that in the beginning, I don't know. It was getting late and if I didn't have her out by 6:00 she'd be stuck for the weekend, and I already knew how expensive that would be. So I rushed to the station, paid the fine and hurried back to the pound, scrambling in the snow with my truck sliding all over, trying to get back by six. I reached the pound at exactly 5:58. Phew, I made it.

When I had to go to court...yes, I actually had to go to court for having a "dog at large", they fined me ten dollars for the first offense. But I wasn't the only criminal dog owner there. The place was almost packed. They really make a big deal out of the leash law in Summit County Colorado (a little fact, just to let you know, if you ever go there and take Fido with you).

Oops......ouch!

Chapter 37

At the time, the leash law technically applied within town limits, but not in the National Forest. There, your dog only had to be under a ten-foot radius voice command. It was something that Jesse didn't quite adhere to unless there was panic in my voice. That didn't happen often, so she stayed relatively close by, and it wasn't a problem. But one time there was a problem.

We were hiking around in our glorious National Forest backyard (yes we were very lucky), and I saw her go off the trail and into the underbrush—which she did on occasion. She was gone for only a moment when we heard a loud yelp. I ran to where she went in and suddenly she came flying out of the brush and was smashing her face to the ground, rubbing her front paws over her face and frantically shaking her head. She had been quilled. Blood was all over her paws, mouth and chest.

I shouted to Carolyn who was farther up the trail, telling her that Jesse had been quilled and we had to run back. So we all headed quickly down the mountain and I rushed Jesse to the vet. Sometimes when a dog gets quilled, you can pull the barbed quills out if you have the right pliers, and they don't have too many quills imbedded in their fur, but Jesse had them both around, and inside her mouth, and all over her chest. Seeing that she was a long white haired dog who was covered with white-ended quills meant that she had to be anaesthetized. Her vet Tom worked for well over an hour pulling out hundreds of quills from Jesse and stitching up her tongue that was ripped apart on the underside from trying to get at the quills. I had to leave her there for a while until she came out of the anesthetic, and when I picked her up, she was still a bit wobbly.

Later that night, the fire department happened to be doing a "practice house burning" drill around the corner and all the neighbors went to watch. These events usually had a big bon fire party atmosphere, but I stayed with my staggering, hurt and confused dog. I felt so sorry for Jesse and hoped she learned her lesson about those innocent but dog-harming creatures we call porcupines.

She was really lucky that she wasn't internally damaged by the quills, as I found out; it's possible. We were headed to Canada about a month later for a family reunion. I was petting her soft head and suddenly felt a sharp sting on my finger. I pulled over to investigate and lo and behold, there was a quill that was barely sticking out of the top of her head. I was able to easily pull it out—the barbs go the way—and looked at it in amazement. Apparently the deeply imbedded barbs that can easily be missed, can travel a path through the body, and come out where they may. This one must have been in the roof of her mouth and came out the top of her head. The one I found about a month later that came out on the side of her body, could have punctured a lung if its path had been so inclined. It's been known to happen in dogs. Yes indeed, we were lucky girls.

Luck was on our side the next summer one time when we were hauling hay. Jesse always rode in the back of the truck and she loved it no matter what. How do I know she loved it this much?

Well, one time many years ago, we were traveling on the highway along the Cumberland Plateau in Tennessee. We were going to help my pastor work on his family's cabin in Mont Eagle. It was absolutely freezing out on this gorgeous sunny day, and originally I wanted to put Jesse inside, but she went around to the back of the truck, telling me that she wanted to ride there, so I let her. Whenever she rode in the back, I checked on her constantly because she had a bad habit of perching on the wheel wells, or balancing her front paws on the side of the truck and leaning on the cab. I was always yelling at her to get down, because I didn't want her to fall, but she usually ignored me and loved to ride this way. I guess it was all the boat cruising experiences that gave her such good balance.

So she was in the back shivering from the cold, but was still leaning into the wind as if it was summer. I finally was tired of all the passers by giving me dirty looks because they felt sorry for my big white polar bear dog, so I pulled over to put her inside. As I was walking her by her collar and was trying to put her into the truck cab, she violently backed away from me, almost pulling clear out of her collar and onto the highway. My heart was in my throat as I grabbed her and pulled her back to the side of the road. I quickly realized that she obviously didn't want to ride inside and tried to calmly walk her to the back of the truck, where she eagerly jumped back into the bed. It had scared me to death when she pulled back away from me, and we never argued about that again.

It would have been a good idea to make a big sign to plaster on my window to ward off the dirty looks: SHE LIKES IT, LEAVE US ALONE!

So she always rode in the back, weather permitting.

Now back to the hay. I had loaded some hay bales in the truck, leaving plenty of room for her in the back, but she insisted on climbing onto the bales until she was in the front, at the top. I kept yelling at her to get down and she'd look at me, but she ignored my requests. Since we were on a two-lane road, without a place to pull over, I slowed down so she'd stay where she was. But we came to a fairly sharp curve and she lost her balance and flipped out of the truck at the exact spot where I had intended to safely pull over to get her inside the cab. I saw the plume of dust in my side view mirror and my heart flew into my throat. I quickly whipped the truck over to the side and was shaking when I hopped out of the truck. I ran back to the site, when a couple came running up, yelling at me.

"Don't you yell at me! I have to find my dog." I shouted to them as I scurried up the side of the hill where she was running through the trees. Maybe she thought I had done this on purpose because I had been yelling at her. Maybe she thought she was in trouble or maybe she was just confused by the whole thing. She wasn't obviously hurt because she kept running, but I caught up to her and was calling her and telling her that it was OK. She eventually stopped. I ran my hands all over her body and she didn't appear to be hurt. I brought her down to the truck and the couple was still there. They started to give me a lecture on the dangers of letting dogs ride in truck beds, but I wasn't in the mood. I told them that I was going to pull over when she fell.

I felt bad enough without having to listen to a lecture, and had already decided that she wouldn't be riding in the back anymore. We went to the ranch to unload the hay, and heard a story about a farm dog who fell out of the truck and was run over by the empty horse trailer. The dog was fine. Tough animals.

When I returned home, I re-checked Jesse before I called the vet and found that she seemed to have landed on her butt and her rectum was a bit flared out and red. I told Tom what had happened and he said to watch her, call him if anything changed, and to give her a bute (a medication for inflammation). She was walking around as if nothing happened, but later was a little stiff, so I gave her another half of a bute tablet. I kept an eye on her through the night. Around three in the morning, she wanted to go out and she walked down the steps just fine. I was relieved, but still took her to Tom in the morning. He said just what I thought. She just barely hurt her butt—nothing really. We were really lucky and she never rode in the back again.

Lady's last day.
Hannah's first of 2 days.

Chapter 38

The day came when my roommate Michael moved out of state. A new gal named Mary Kathryn moved in with us, and she just loved Jesse right away. She thought Jesse was the funniest dog she had ever met. Because Jesse was a bread thief and a beer drinker, because she did such silly things, or because Jesse kissed her; I wasn't sure. Jesse wasn't a licker at all—something I was certainly grateful for, but that also meant that she rarely gave kisses; except to a few select people. I wasn't one of them.

Jesse really liked Mary Kathryn too and she showed it. Sometimes when we were hanging out in the living room talking, we'd test Jesse just for kicks. I'd try to have Jesse give me a kiss. I'd sit on the floor, make Jesse sit next to me and lean in to have her give me a kiss on my cheek. "C'mon Jesse, give me a kiss. C'mon Jess."

But every single time she'd turn her head and look away like a movie star posing for an 8x10 glossy. Mary Kathryn would start laughing and Jesse would stroll over to her and give her a facial bath with her huge tongue, and then look back at me. She also did this with my sister—who got a big kick out of it too. I didn't think it was funny at all.

Yes, Jesse was a brat at times and when she took off to roam the neighborhood one snowy winter night, I wasn't too happy with her. I started to follow the tracks, as I had done years earlier in Denver, but didn't go too far when I realized what she was doing...again. Even though the Animal Control Patrol is much stricter in Summit County than probably anywhere in the world, I decided that they too, have a day job. I went in and awaited her arrival. When she returned and knocked at the patio door, I let her in and pretended she had just gone out to pee. In all the years we lived together, I finally learned not to make a big deal out of things—it just didn't matter. She still did as she pleased. Little miss independent.

"You can't teach an old dog new tricks." Not true. Jesse didn't learn any tricks when she was young—she had too much of an attitude. But when she was about eleven years old, I saw the biscuit-on-the-nose trick on TV and thought, hmmmm, would Jesse do that? She's smart and she loves treats. So I called her into the kitchen, balanced a biscuit on her nose and told her to wait. She sat there looking at me as if I was from Pluto, but when I said OK, she flipped it right into her mouth. Wow, she was good. We tried it a few more times with the same results. She was a biscuit pro, but in later times she missed every now and then. Guess the pros do too.

I used to love watching professional football and especially The Superbowl. But it was always a hard day for Jesse.

She had moments of frustration whenever I watched TV. If she went to the door to be let out and it was in the middle of a movie or program, I told her, "Wait for a commercial Jesse, wait for a commercial." (Of course if she really had to go out—I let her out.) So she learned to lie back down until she heard the louder noise coming from the TV, which was usual for commercials, then she'd head for the door. But if I was watching the Superbowl at home with a few friends, Jesse's established TV-watching behavior was sadly disrupted. Due to the fact that for some reason, the Superbowl usually isn't a closely-played game, the real entertainment lies in the commercials. Poor Jesse. She'd get up to go out when she heard the louder noise of the commercials, and I'd tell her, "Wait for the game Jesse, wait for the game."

She'd go and lie down again, muttering about the stupid commercials. She hated Superbowl Sunday.

Because Jesse was such an easy going dog around dogs, sometimes we were able to help friends by ranch sitting, and times by dog-sitting and keeping dogs at our house. This par-ticular time we were doing a combination of both.

My pal Wayne had asked me if I'd watch his German shep-herd named Lady for a couple of days when he was out of town. Sure, no problem. Then some friends asked if I'd watch their ranch. I usually ranch sat for them and said that was fine, but I'd have another female dog with me for one overlapping day and night at the end of their week. They said that was OK, since their Dalmatian named Oreo was male. There probably wouldn't be any problems.

Jesse and I stayed out at the ranch for the week and then on the second to last day, Wayne came out and dropped Lady off to stay with us. Oreo and Lady got along fine and things were swell. That last night was a beautiful fall night and I remember sitting on the fence looking at the moon and thinking about going for a ride.

Horseback riding is one of my favorite things to do, and there have been a few doozies in the accident department, but I usually stick with the horse and get crunched. Well, that wasn't the case this night. Jeff had a very stout appaloosa named Major who was a well trained horse, but I made the mistake of trying to get him to go away from the herd at a run. When he cut back at a ninety degree angle, I was wrapped around his neck—only to come crashing to the ground and landing on my head. I got knocked out. I know this, because when I got up and went to get Major, he was sound asleep by the gate to the pasture, and I saw that my coat was covered with blood. I had the thought of "getting back on when you get bucked off" but my head was pounding so hard that I just unsaddled Major, put him back in the pasture, had a shower to wash my head and went to bed. I put a bag of ice on the pillow and slept on it.

I didn't know it was a rather stupid thing to do. I found out later that you're not supposed to go to sleep when you've been knocked out. I ended up with a pretty heavy-duty concussion and headaches for quite a while, but once again the Good Lord had watched after me. The next day was my last at the ranch, so I packed up Jesse and Lady and returned home.

I spent Thursday nursing my head and trying to relax while getting ready for a meeting I had in Denver on Friday morning. I'd have to leave the dogs alone for about six hours and didn't think it'd be a problem. But when I got home and opened the door, the scene was worthy of a *Columbo* episode.

Lady had gone berserk and ransacked our apartment like a burglar looking for a microchip. She didn't have to go out—she had conveniently used one area as her toilet, and then stepped in it numerous times and tracked it all around the apartment. And I mean everywhere. All the blinds were torn down from the windows, floor plants were overturned, the carpet was covered with dirt, furniture was knocked over, upset lamps lying on the floor. Mary Kathryn's CD rack was capsized when Lady obviously tried to get out of the closed window, after her poop-clad paw tore down the blind. It was a nightmare. I was in shock. It didn't do wonders for my concussion either. What was Jesse doing while this psycho was ransacking the place? I just couldn't picture her helping with this disaster. It really wasn't her style. She probably just sat, watched, and wondered what would happen later. But I would venture to guess that she coached Lady in the art of looking innocent—as she had done so many times when the bread was missing.

Well, I cleaned up the mess slowly and painfully and then rested. I didn't know what to do with Lady. I wanted to ship her to Japan in a can. Mary Kathryn couldn't believe the photos of the devastation. I never watched that dog again.

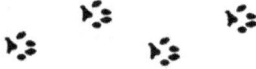

But I didn't give up helping my friends if they went out of town and needed someone to watch their inside animals, as well as the outside ones. One place where Jesse and I stayed had a dog, two iguanas, a bird, a donkey and two horses. Everything was going along just swell, until one afternoon I went to put the bigger iguana back into his cage and he was gone. I looked high and low for the reptile, to no avail. Since I had to work that night and it was very cold out, I left the dogs inside.

I fretted about this renegade iguana the whole time I was at work and when I was off, I sped home, hoping to find him basking on the couch. Nope, he wasn't. I scoured the house for him and was worried because he was supposed to be in the temperature-controlled cage. I finally gave up and headed to bed. I awoke in the middle of the night with the most horrible thought; Jesse! She ate the iguana! I was sure of it. She had eaten rabbits, rabbit pelts, foxes, fox pelts, tin foil, candle wax, shoes, clothes, you name it—so why not an iguana? I hardly slept for the rest of the night and even examined Jesse's belly as she lay sleeping, knowing that the iguana was the big bulge. I impatiently waited for morning, when Jesse went to the bathroom, and followed her outside in my slippers and robe, oblivious of the frigid air, intent on checking her poop—hoping and praying there wouldn't be any green scales anywhere. My imagination must have gotten the best of me because there wasn't a green scale to be found, but neither was the iguana. He never showed up. Months later (I actually think it was about a year later), I had the courage to ask Pauline if they ever found the iguana. She said yes, they found him. He was petrified. I asked, "What was he afraid of?"

"No Patti, he was petrified—like a rock."

Oops.

The iguana was a goner and Jesse almost was too. One day Mary Lou and her kids Drew and Lea came out to ride during that same animal sitting adventure. Jesse was milling around while we were saddling the horses, and the donkey was hanging around in the background. When we mounted up, suddenly the donkey started to attack Jesse for no reason at all. He ran after her, rearing and crashing down near her, striking out at her. I watched in horror. Because I had Lea with me in the saddle and couldn't risk her falling off if we chased after the donkey, I was helpless to do anything but yell, "Run Jesse run!" Even though Jesse wasn't a youngster anymore, she found the ability to dodge the angry hooves and take cover by a car. I was shaking when we reached the donkey to herd him away from Jesse, and I dismounted to calm my scared little buddy. We were able to keep the tyrant away while we passed through the gate to safety. The times I was afraid for Jesse's life weren't quite the same, and thankfully I never feared *that* way again.

Peejo

Chapter 39

Jesse however did fear for her life when she got into the garbage. But she just couldn't help it. They all do it at some point, but I hated when that happened. My happy tail-wagging dog didn't come to the door welcoming me home when she had just had a trip to the scrumptious smorgasbord we call garbage, and it was hard to teach her not to do it because I never caught her at it. She did it when she was alone and she was good at it, but she wasn't neat about it. If you have a garbage dog, you can relate.

They say if you pile all the garbage on them and make them sit there for a while, it will make them stop this annoying activity. So I tried it, making sure that things were piled high on Jesse's paws, because she hated when her paws were touched by anything. (Nail clipping was an absolute nightmare—you'd think I was killing her from the howls she screamed.) The goal was for her to be so uncomfortable and squirmy that she would never get into the garbage again. It didn't work.

It just doesn't work for some dogs. Jesse's friend Peejo loves to get into the garbage. My friend B came home one day to find that once again, Peejo had been into the trash. So B piled everything on and around Peejo and took a picture. It hangs on the fridge. It's a funny photo and we humans get a kick out of it. Peejo walks by and remembers, "Oh yeah, that was a great day. I went to the buffet and when Mom got home, I got to go again! She let me. It was fun. I didn't think I got all the cream cheese out of that wrapper."

By the way, the pile-up method didn't work for Peejo either. She's still a trash dog.

Another remedy I've heard of somewhere is to put cayenne pepper around the garbage container and the heat of the pepper will deter them from getting into the garbage. Well, sounds like a good idea and it probably works for some dogs, but when their mom loves Chernobyl-caliber food, it doesn't work. Sometimes I make extremely hot and spicy chicken wings, and I finally learned to wrap up and dispose of the bones in a very high place, because if I didn't take these pre-cautions, old iron stomach Jesse would get into the garbage and clean out the whole pile of bones. This was the dog who ate candle wax, aluminum foil and wallpaper paste as a pup, so yummy, fiery, burn your stomach, chicken wing bones was a real treat.

It's not fair for me to say that all dogs get into the garbage. Some might not be able to reach it, although there's probably that Olympic Dachshund out there who can. Maybe the garbage is so well hidden, they don't even try. Oh, that would be torture. "I can smell it. I can smell it. I just can't find it."

Or maybe they really are that good dog who has self-control over that particularly strong impulse. You people with the perfect dogs probably know all about that.

Well, my garbage can was generally out, Jesse was a tall dog, and self-control wasn't part of her personality, so she never had any problem getting into the trash. I couldn't hide the garbage because we usually lived in old houses where cabinet space was limited, which is actually a moot point because she'd open the cabinet doors anyway. Once I came home to find the Comet container, which lived next to the garbage can behind a closed door, sitting upright on the kitchen floor, while the tipped over garbage can sat next to it. There was garbage everywhere. I have no idea how she managed that one.

But getting into the garbage wasn't a daily, weekly, or even monthly event, it was sporadic. Looking back, it was just when something especially pungent was in the trash and she just had to have it. I eventually quit trying to get her to stop this pain in the butt behavior and just gave up. I'd come home, see the mess, sigh heavily, yell at Jesse under my breath and begin cleaning up the grossness that was scattered all around the kitchen. Somehow, I don't think I am alone in this.

But I'm probably alone in this: I sometimes skin "road kill". For anyone who has a weak stomach you'll want to skip this part.

I started doing this when me 'n Jess lived back home in Park Ridge, Illinois. On my way home one day, the car in front of me passed over a fox squirrel that was dead in the road. The air that flew by the tiny body as the car sped over, made the tail fly up to reveal a beautiful pattern of yellow, red and black fur. Suddenly, I knew I had to have the tail. I pulled onto a side street and walked over to the still warm animal. I picked the squirrel up by the tail and carefully placed it in my truck bed.

A hunter friend of mine helped me with this project. He asked if I wanted the whole pelt and not just the tail. Yeah, great. You might be wondering why I would want the tail to begin with. Well, I'm not exactly sure, to be honest. Maybe it's due to my interest in Native American's use of pelts, or the fact that I dislike seeing squished animals in the road or that I hate waste of any kind, I don't know. But I do know that I'd rather see a beautiful pelt on my wall than be part of a heap on the road that I'd have to pass for weeks.

Well, when I first moved back to Colorado, I was riding my motorcycle on my way to visit my pal Mary Lou, and passed a tiny chipmunk that had been hit. I picked it up, put it in the small outside pocket of my backpack, and headed to Silverthorne. After a lovely catch up visit, I told Mary Lou that I had to be going. I explained why and showed her the dead chipmunk, when she exclaimed, "Oh, the kids would love to see you skin it, they could learn something."

"Are you sure they wouldn't be grossed out?"

She assured me the kids would be fine. So we set up a table outside in the fresh mountain air and with the sun beating its warmth onto our backs, I started to skin this petite animal with a drafter's blade- while four young children observed. They were enthralled as they watched me open up this small critter. They leaned closely to the chipmunk, watching my every move, while little Madeline kept a slow but fairly steady chant: "The poor poor little squir-rel. The poor poor little squir-rel. He's dead."

Yup he was.

At first, the eight-year-old boys were very interested and Drew helped me by holding the pelt taut while I worked, but they soon lost interest and merely checked on my progress. The two young girls however never left the table once; they watched, asked questions and commented on the chipmunk. When I accidentally pierced the abdominal cavity and a bit of blood flowed out, Madeline changed her chant: "The poor poor little squir-rel. He's really dead now."

"Well, he's always been dead, but I guess you're right, he's really dead now," I chuckled at the four year old logic. Blood meant real death. When I was finished, I explained that I had to take the pelt home to salt it—to preserve it and to take away any smell. Mary Lou thanked me for giving her kids the crash biology lesson. I carefully loaded the pelt into my pack and headed home.

Drew ended up becoming a fellow skinner when he was older—as well as my competition for the critters on the road. His early-to-rise dad spotted the animals that now adorn Drew's walls instead of mine. Oh well.

What does all of this have to do with Jesse? Well, one night while I was living in Park Ridge with my mom, and was up a tree, putting the Christmas lights around the branches, Jesse was chasing a rabbit in the yard. I heard the commotion, saw the bunny scamper away and yelled, "Get Jess! Mum, don't let her get the rabbit!" as I saw Jesse bury her nose under a piece of wood that was leaning against the fence.

Mum spun around, but wasn't near enough to Jesse. "I can't get to her," she cried.

Mum had been handing the lights to me with a broom and I wanted her to block Jesse's path with it. "Use the broom! Stop her with the broom!"

But when I heard the short piercing squeal, I knew it was too late. Jesse came out with the bunny hanging from her mouth like a big rag and walked warily along the fence, looking like a lioness in a National Geographic special. I had jumped down from my perch in the tree during all of this and walked over to Jesse.

"Give me the bunny."

"Nope."

"Jesse. Give me the bunny."

"Nope. It's mine."

"You can't eat a bunny here in this yard."

"Why not? I caught it."

"This is a suburb of Chicago Jesse, not the jungle. Give me the bunny."

"But it's mine."

"I know Jess, and I'm sorry, but you can't have it here."

"Aw, Mom."

She was very reluctant to surrender her prize, but it just didn't seem right, and besides, I wanted the pelt.

Paybacks are... well, you know. While driving home one cold winter evening in Colorado, I found a snowshoe hare lying by the side of the road. I was able to get a very pretty pelt—including the beautiful black tipped ears—out of the poor rabbit, and it hung proudly on the wall in my breezeway. It stayed there peacefully displayed, until one day Jesse had a flashback of her rabbit prize I had taken from her. She tore the white rabbit pelt off the wall and ate it. I was really mad at her. My white pelt was a lot harder to come by than the plain old gray pelt I had taken from her bunny. I never took another prize away from her.

Chapter 40

Airline seat designers sure don't deserve a prize for comfort. You can relate if you've ever flown coach from Denver to London, or any long trans-oceanic trip. And Heathrow has a funny system of letting you know about the gate status for your connecting flight. Every time you check the sign for your gate, for example gate 5, it says "wait in the lounge", and then in a split second, it changes to "Gate 5. Gate closing." Your heart starts pounding, so you hightail it to the gate, only to have to wait for another half hour, while trying to catch your breath as the rivers of sweat are cascading down your back and your clothes are clinging to you like a scared cat to a tree. Maybe it's their way of forcing you to loosen the muscles that have turned to cement during the flight, I don't know, but once you know their secret, you can mosey along to the gate without panic.

It was November 14, 2000 when the cab brought me back to Greenane and I couldn't believe I was actually there. It was surreal to me, seeing the boats, the sea, and the lights of the houses on the hillsides. I could write a whole book about my adventure in Ireland, but will share only a few of the highlights.

I vowed not to go to a pub for the first week or more, because I didn't want to run into Danny until he knew I was there and had adjusted to the idea. But Sean convinced me that it would be best if I went right away, and then stayed away. OK sure. So we went to a pub where Danny would not be and ran into his best friend instead. This was good. Danny would know immediately that I was back.

Leaving the pub, I took the shore walk and ended up sitting thoughtfully and calmly on a rock—watching the waves that sparkled in the moonlight softly lap against the black rocks of the shore. I smiled. It was exhilarating and comforting at the same time. I was excited and nervous about being there, but felt a peaceful feeling inside. I was supposed to be in Greenane. The sea drew me in, and I started a three-month-long routine of taking the shore walk any time of day or night, no matter how far away I lived.

Time out for an important tangent. It has to do with the fact that I'm so very grateful that I can walk. Because of a terrible horse accident I had on January 7, 1999, I almost lost my left leg from the knee down.

I want to share this story because it was a miraculous event and if it hadn't happened there's a chance this book still wouldn't exist.

It was a picture-perfect wintry day and my friend Bruce and I went riding behind my house on Ptarmigan Mountain. He was riding his palomino mare named Scuffies. I was riding Jimmy (my three year old buckskin gelding). The sun was reflecting its bright rays on the fresh white snow, the sky was the typical brilliant blue that occurs often in the Colorado Rockies, and the mountains looked especially bright and crisp. We were on our way back down, heading home after a beautiful ride. We had already walked over the hidden ice flow that was caused by the creek and changing temperatures that we'd been having, but we didn't know it was there—until now. I had a habit of taking my feet out of the stirrups on this part of the trail because it's pretty steep, and it's a good thing I did. We rounded the bend and I was thinking, "Jimmy, be careful", when suddenly he lost his footing. His legs collapsed beneath him and he scrambled to try to get up, but over the side we flew. We crashed to the side of the hill from above and Jimmy landed squarely on my left leg. My leg was sandwiched between rock-hard ice, a rock-hard stirrup, and nine hundred-plus pounds of horse flesh. I remember thinking; THAT HURT!! He somehow was able to get his legs underneath him, and he pushed up and we flipped over to the side, smashing my helmet-clad head into a tree. THAT HURT! I fell to the ground on my stomach and careened down the ice, sliding along with Jimmy, who was now ahead of me. At least I think he was, I'm not exactly sure. I remember the violent smashing into trees and underbrush that my body was doing—completely out of control. I felt like a pinball crashing here and bouncing there and flipping all over the place. It happened so incredibly fast. I somehow flipped again, probably hitting the tree that Jimmy ended up being wedged under, and I was in a pile between Jimmy's legs. We stopped. Oh. I felt like Dorothy at the end of the tornado scene in the "Wizard of Oz".

Patricia A. White

I've had a few horse accidents in the past and for some reason have a bad habit of jumping right up. I did then too—after pulling my right leg out from underneath Jimmy's belly. I knew immediately that my left leg was in really bad shape, but seeing Jimmy lying there, trapped underneath the tree, I had no thought of myself. Thinking back, it was an absolute miracle that I was able to move at all. Crashing over the side of an ice flow, sliding down the ice, flipping around with a nine hundred pound horse and taking out aspen trees as we went, it's amazing that I didn't break my back or neck—especially when my head smashed into the tree. I know my guardian angel was with us that day. Actually, I believe that God probably sent down a whole committee of them for us.

My very first thought was; "chainsaws, we'll need chainsaws to get Jimmy out." My second thought was Animal Planet Rescues that I had seen once on TV. I yelled to Bruce who was up on the trail, "We're really in trouble here Bruce."

"Are you OK!?" He shouted from the trail, his voice shaking and full of panic. I couldn't see him yet, because he apparently had to go down the trail to turn around because it was so tight and steep there. But when he was able to see us, he saw me throwing small trees and brush off of Jimmy. He had seen us flip over the side, heard me scream and thought one of us was dead. He was relieved and wanted to help, but since there wasn't a place to tie his horse and it was too icy for them to come down, I was on my own.

I was amazingly calm as I assessed the situation and knew what I had to do. Shock does that to a person. Jimmy didn't seem to be hurt, so of course I was very relieved and happy. He raised his head to look at me when I stood behind him reaching for the rein clips, then he gently put it down and moaned a long agonizing moan. I talked to him softly and told him he'd be all right and somehow he seemed to relax and became passive about our pinball ride we had survived. I undid the rein clips first, because there was a branch sticking out between his face and the reins, and I didn't want him to get cut if he moved. I had to go back around to his belly to undo the tightened cinch, and even though I knew I was standing in the wrong spot if he moved, it was the only way to get to the cinch and the breast collar. I was so lucky that Jimmy's a smart horse and he trusted me. Usually when a horse is pinned down, they thrash their legs to try to get up, because they panic and are afraid. If he had been most horses whom I have known, he would have kicked my legs out from under me and I'd have been toast. It was very lucky he didn't thrash and nail me when I was in a heap between his legs in the first place.

I was finally able to undo the cinch, and walked back around and freed his tangled tail from the brush so it didn't pull him down when he tried to get up. I stood above him and tried to pull the binding saddle away from him, but realized that it was wedged too tightly, so I went down and around to his back legs. He had to be pulled down hill. I now know how old ladies can move cars to free a pinned child. Adrenaline and shock are amazing. I grabbed his legs, but hesitated for a split second and thought, "He has such cute little legs." A silly "in shock" thought I assume. I then proceeded to pull him down about three feet. I walked back around to stand above him, I freed the saddle and checked all around him before I told him it was OK to get up. He slowly lifted his head and then tried to get his feet underneath him, but he slipped on the ice. My heart skipped, thinking "NOW he's broken a leg." But he didn't. Then he proceeded to do something that I have never seen a horse do: he stood half way up, but then crouched down low, and he dug his hooves into the ice using his toes like ice picks, and clambered his way up the steep slope.

I looked up at him and felt immense relief. He was safe and seemingly unhurt. He slowly turned his head to look down at me as if to ask, "Mom, what are you doing down there?" then he licked his lips (a sign of acceptance and comfort for a horse), and I knew he was fine. It was a miracle.

I stood down in the gully and yelled to Bruce, who was on the homeward side of the slippery ice flow. I told him that we were going to be fine. I looked back at Jimmy, who was still standing there and told him that it was OK, he could walk around. He looked towards Bruce and Scuffies and knew where he should go. I watched in utter amazement. He carefully crossed the creek bed, but before he came to the spot where we slipped, he gave it a very questioning look, walked up onto the hillside to skirt the danger zone, and then came back down when he reached Bruce. I just couldn't believe how smart and relaxed he was acting. He was only a three-year-old at the time, just a kid.

I limped up the hill to join the bunch grabbing the saddle and pad as I went. Bruce hugged me with relief and I hugged Jimmy fiercely and was so thankful for my wonderful horse. When we were putting the saddle and breast collar back on Jimmy, I incidentally touched him on the chest, a special cue, and he did his "hello" trick. "How could you think about treats at a time like this?" I hugged him again. "You could have been killed!" I smiled to him, giving him a treat from my pocket. I wondered if Jesse was in there somewhere...

So we both walked out and away from an incredible accident and I ended up missing only about four months of work. I came close to losing my leg below the knee, by getting a touch of compartmental syndrome—that's when the injured part of the body shuts off from the rest of the body and won't heal. But I was so very fortunate. Blood clots, gangrene, infection, anything remotely wrong and goodbye leg, but my leg survived. It's slightly deformed and discolored, but hey, it's there!

After three weeks of lying around with my leg elevated and trying to get better, I ended up going home to Illinois to be with family. Living on a mountainside in ice and snow without water, and not being able to walk was a bit much. It made sense for me to go home to heal. I couldn't walk, but I could drive. So I drove for the first time in a while. I was actually a little nervous because I had to go down to Denver on the Sunday night after the Broncos won the Superbowl, and there were mini riots in the streets. I just drove slowly past the wild people who were running around like maniacs. I smiled and returned their shouts. GO BRONCOS! NUMBER ONE!

My friend Bob took me to the airport the next day and the flight home was fine. I was glad to be at my mom's house. That first night, Mum and I were sitting on her bed talking.

"I was thinking that maybe we could go to see Nanny this weekend since you're here." My mom said looking at my leg that was high on pillows. Nanny was my grandma up in Canada who was living in an assisted living home near my mom's sister in Owen Sound, Ontario.

"That's a great idea Mum. I think my leg would make it."

"Well, let's see how the week goes."

"Sounds like a plan."

"If not then, maybe in the spring. Nanny's as strong as a horse. She's not going anywhere."

Well two days later, Nanny fell out of bed and broke her neck. She died late that Saturday night, but not before Mum was able to catch a plane and get up to her bedside. I was glad I was there to help Mum out when she was throwing things together to go in a flash, and to take her to the airport.

The whole family was sad and in shock.

I had always said that I didn't want to go to Nanny's funeral. I wanted to remember Nanny as she was. Now I was going to her funeral. I thought in my way of trying to figure out why things happen, "I know I'm stubborn Lord, but did you have to drop a horse on me to make me go to the funeral!?" But maybe I knew...

I'm not saying that God does bad things directly to us, because He doesn't. But I was just trying, in my humanness, to find a reason for that life-changing event. But we know that God uses all things for good, according to His purposes, it's just that we may never know what that purpose is.

OK, long tangent over—but it really is amazing to me...still.

So that's the story about the close call I had and why I'm so grateful to be walking. And I did a lot of walking in Ireland. The shore walk was calming, even in the storms, and the pier was always changing with the boats coming and going. The Irish fishing industry is very interesting. There are many different types of boats used specifically for fishing for various types of fish. The large mussel dredgers that can hold one hundred tons of mussels, the small oyster boats, and the massive white fish vessels that venture far out to sea are just a few. The pier was a peaceful place to walk and I loved listening to the sounds of the vessels as they shifted and rocked gently with the waves. The creaking of the wood, the scent of the sea and the brightly colored boats with interesting names created a sense of tranquility that I cherished.

I stayed with Sean and Briana for a while and then rented my own flat. I needed to have my own space to think and write. It worked out well and my days were spent writing and walking and sometimes I'd go to the pubs in the evenings. I met loads of the friendly townsfolk and enjoyed hearing stories about the area and the people.

After being there for a week and a half, Thanksgiving rolled around and I went to Sean's to visit them and use their phone to call my family to wish them a Happy Thanksgiving. They were anxious about my adventure, but I calmed their fears. I was supposed to be there.

Afterward, I decided that now it was OK if I ran into Danny. I headed to O'Malley's Pub with my stomach in huge knots. I thought there'd be a lot of people inside, judging by the number of cars outside, but I opened the door to see that there were only two patrons sitting at the bar. Liam and Danny. I looked right into Danny's eyes and I'm sure major shock registered on my face. But I cowboyed up, sat at the bar and had a pint with the boys. Danny asked about Scotland and my travels, and I tried to calm my heart's wild beating through conversation. It was very hard to do, when I'd look into the eyes of this man who had me all messed up, but I survived the first meeting and figured that everything was going to be fine.

Kenya, Rusty and Jesse.

Chapter 41

Everything was going along just fine, living at 510 Belford in Summit County, until one day the owners sold the building and we had to move. Crap! We have to find a new place again. I didn't know exactly what we were going to do, but a few days later when I was sitting talking to B at the Moosejaw (where she worked), our buddy Pete came in. I told him what was happening and he told me that they were looking for someone to live in the back part of the house he was in. He used to live there before, but there was a fire. Now it had been rebuilt and was almost ready for a renter. Because he and his buddy Mark had moved into the front of the big house, the back was open. I was very excited because his spot was one of the coolest places in the county.

So I drove up to go and talk to Larry the landlord who was still working on the finishing details at the house. We all hit it off immediately. Jesse and I were in.

We had to wait until after Labor Day weekend to move in, and a caravan of seven pickup truck loads later, Jesse and I were living in paradise. It was on the highest road on Ptarmigan Mountain and was the third house from the top. The views of the Gore Range, The Ten Mile Range, the Continental Divide and Dillon Reservoir were spectacular. My friends in Frisco used to call me to find out what the weather was 10 miles up the valley to the north, so they'd know what to expect for horseback riding. We could see everything for miles and miles around.

Yes indeed, it was heaven—that is, if you don't count the road. It was a very steep and rocky road that I plummeted down backwards many times on the ice and snow, and it wasn't fun at all—especially when I was hauling close to a ton of water.

Jesse and I didn't have water. Not running water. But the boys had two 700 gallon cisterns in the garage that held water for the front part of the house and they had a pump system. They had a working kitchen sink and a full bathroom complete with a bathtub. Jesse and I on the hand didn't even have a pipe. So I set up our own systems. I bought two 35 gallon cans; a seven gallon container with a spicket, and a bucket for the kitchen; and a porta-potty that I could empty into the outhouse. We were set. We hauled our water from town and whenever I brought water up the mountain for me 'n Jess, I always put the extra in the boy's tanks in case I needed an emergency shower. (I usually showered at work.)

Jesse loved the new living arrangement. She didn't have to be tied up, could roam around in the backyard—that was the side of the mountain, and she had two new friends; Rusty and Kenya. They were both golden retrievers, but were different colors. Rusty was Pete's dog and his coat was a beautiful deep red color. Kenya was Mark's dog and she was very golden. The three made a colorful bunch and they became great pals.

Jesse especially loved when hunting season rolled around. Now that we lived with hunters, when they were successful,

Jesse had a heyday with the elk and deer legs. She had always loved gnawing on them and had developed a knack of finding them off the trails where we used to hike. She'd bring them along with her until I'd make her give them up because of the smell (remember the cow leg at Percy Priest Lake?), but now she had fresh ones to enjoy and she didn't even have to go and find them herself; they were delivered right to her door. It was a curious thing that she loved to chew on the raw meat, but when she smelled it cooking, it freaked her out. Weird.

We both loved living on the mountainside and I liked the fact that when I had to leave her, she was happy to stay on the hill and chase chipmunks. We used to ride the horses up to the house, and she never followed us down; her hiking days were over and she knew it. Her back legs shook too much if we went on a long hike, so she was content to hang out at the house with Kenya. She was getting older and had slowed down some, but everyone who met her guessed her age to be around eight or nine because she was still peppy. And since she had always been white, her face didn't change as she aged, like the cinnamon-and-salt style of most golden retrievers.

I always said, "If Jesse makes it to be thirteen years old, I'll have a party for her." She did. So I did. The invitations went out to all her best friends, asking them to tell their mom or dad to dress warmly because it would be a bonfire party, and to BYOB: bring your own biscuits. Conveniently, her October

28th birthday fell on a Saturday, so about twelve or thirteen dogs showed up, as well as a pack of humans, and it was a grand affair. Most of the dogs were willing to join in the celebration by wearing and leaving their hats on, but there were a few who didn't tolerate the cone hats Jesse was giving out to her guests.

Peejo and B brought her a meat pie and Karen brought her a wreath made of dog treats. She was smiling gratefully while she snarfed them down. There were a few fights over sticks, but Jesse was too busy lapping up beer to notice the commotion. One romance developed between Rusty and Pebbles (Bruce's Australian shepherd). Rusty followed her absolutely everywhere and draped his head over her back or shoulder, but he was such a gentleman, never trying any funny business. It was a beautiful one night courtship.

The party was a success, Jess turned thirteen, and there were only a couple of hangovers to be had. Remember Hannah the party girl?

Ours was a non-typical winter that first year living on Ptarmigan Mountain. It snowed twenty-nine of thirty-one days in January and we were snowed in for eight days. I was on foot because of making the mistake of not moving my truck down to the trailhead parking lot below, but it worked out fine with friends giving me rides to town from there.

Jesse and I took short hikes on the sunny days that followed the dreary month of January and we were in a winter wonderland. The amazing deep blue skies and the beautiful sun-glitter of the snow that covered the mountains were so magical to enjoy. I was glad the scenery was so incredible because I wasn't thrilled with the fact that I never knew if I'd make it home after work if it was snowing, or if I'd go careening backwards at the speed of sound headed towards the cliff. But my old Dodge did a pretty good job most of the time.

It was a long winter that year. One of the best "powder days" was May second. It was Carolyn's birthday and we went skiing on a beautiful sunny day. There were lots of people at A Basin and I can honestly remember experiencing such a joyous feeling that spring day as we all seemed so grateful to live in such a wonderful place.

The snow took its sweet time melting, but summer finally arrived. Me 'n Jess were glad we made it through our first winter on the mountainside, and now it was time for horseback riding, relaxing on the mountain, day trips and hiking. Camping was especially great because conveniently, since there was so much snow that year, there were storage refrigerators everywhere in the high country on the shaded northern sides of many of the trees. It was a fun summer.

Wicklow Mountains

Chapter 42

It's interesting that Northern Ireland doesn't contain the most northern place in Ireland. Malin Head, at the top of Ireland is in the Republic of Ireland, on the Inishowen Peninsula. I had previously been around the peninsula but one day my new friends Avril and Peter took me to Malivey Bay, a very peaceful spot in Inishowen. Stir-crazy from sitting and writing for most of the days and evenings (having worked in restaurants for twenty years and being used to running and being around people), it was hard to stand this business of sitting around. It was a fun day and I was glad to be away from Greenane for the afternoon.

I walked the shore walk at some point in every twenty-four hour period, and taking it at three or four in the morning was my favorite time. It was thought provoking and I loved watching the always-changing sea. The frigid nights when the moon was bright, the water was calm, and the waves were soft feathers of water tickling the shore, contrasted the stormy nights when the waves smashed against the rocks, sending white plumes of water high into the air. Because I'd be returning to my beloved mountains, absorbing as much of the sea and the life it offers to others, was the intention of these daily shore walks.

The creaking and moaning of the boats at the pier as they nestled against each after a day of dredging the lough for mussels, or being far out to sea in search of white fish, was a mesmerizing sound. I was curious about the whole fishing industry—having served many a fish on a platter, and wanted to go out on a boat to watch how it was done, but never had the chance. Not that they really believed the bad luck thing; that was just a good excuse... But I didn't mind too much because being prone to motion sickness, heaving over the side of a boat wasn't my idea of a fun day in Ireland.

There were many fun days though. Despite working on a book, I felt like I was on holidays. And I was hoping to lose some facial wrinkles with all the humidity and water there, but since I spent so much of the time laughing, I added more. I was at Kearnan's pub one Sunday afternoon when my friend Colleen said this about someone; "No wonder she doesn't have any wrinkles, she never laughs!" And most of those people sure do laugh. A lot.

It really felt like home there because most mountain people tend to be laid-back and not bothered by many things, and the Irish on the whole, seem to be the same. Even though technology is quickly catching up and there is major growth and building, they still have a relaxed attitude towards life. "No panic." is a favorite saying.

Another favorite is; "I'm going to the pub for a pint." It doesn't happen. Period. You can NOT go to the pub for A pint. Someone always buys you another. It's just the way it is. The pubs are the social scene. People don't usually drink at home or at their friends' houses like they do in the States or Canada—they go out to the pubs. That's where they learn about what's going on in the town, on the farms, or out at sea. It's just the way of the Irish.

Irish customs about death and funerals are interesting—and entertaining. They still practice the custom of having the wake in the person's home. There aren't many funeral homes around, except in the bigger metropolitan areas, so they "wake" the person, generally for three days, and then they carry the coffin to the church. As the procession is going down the street, the family walks closest to the coffin and friends follow behind. Some of the people who live in houses there, will come out and stand watching, and many will join in. If the church is miles away, everyone drives to the church for the service. Since most of the graveyards are close to the church, they carry the coffin on foot to be put into the ground, and then they say their farewells. After the burial, they all go out to the pubs and celebrate that person's life. I think they have the right idea about life and death...and I was around for a few fun funerals.

Aside from seeing familiar faces at the funerals, I sometimes met up with Sean at O'Malley's or Avril and Peter at

Kearnan's and would often run into Danny. We sat and talked a lot about many things including America, which I don't think he will ever see. Fishermen are their own breed. They live in another world—especially when they've lived in the same town all their life. It's a rough life being called out in an instant to fish if the waters change or load the haul if the shipping trucks come in at a different time than planned. Fishing at all times of the night or day and for many days at a time. Yes it's a tough way to make a living, even if it can be a good living.

It was a mystery to me why I kept seeing Danny at odd times of the day, and only because we happened to be in a certain place at a certain time. There weren't any patterns to either of our activities, yet there he was, all around the town. I even knew that he was ill one day when he rode by in his car. The feeling washed over me like a bucket of cold water—I just knew something was wrong and found out later, there was. It was strange. But I was gratefully able to spend time with him, talking by ourselves. I had to try to get answers as to why he had such a hold on my heart... why I felt such a mysterious connection. We incidentally saw each at the pub the night before I left for Killarney for the Holidays to be with Pete and Eve, and I was happy for the chance to talk to him and spend time with him before going away for three weeks. (There had been a funeral that day, so the pub was packed.) It was a great time that night laughing and talking with Danny and enjoying his company, along with a bunch of the town folk. It was a grand send-off for the Holidays.

I spent Christmas in Killarney with Pete and Eve, and as the ole Bing Crosby song goes, we had a wonderful time. Actually we were in Kenmare, but kept singing the Killarney song anyway. It was a beautiful area of Ireland with mountains and farms everywhere and this year, we were snowed in. It was the first time in ten years since they had snow, and it was the worst snow storm since 1964. And we were there. How grand. We felt right at home. We enjoyed the snow and walked around the countryside but didn't dare get on the roads. They were bad. And we certainly didn't want to discover how terrible the drivers were in the snow; they were like NASCAR drivers on the dry roads.

We thought since the roads were so bad, we wouldn't be able to go out for New Year's Eve, but thankfully, the rain and wind came and melted all the snow. To see the snow disappear overnight was pretty amazing because in the mountains of Colorado, the snow stays from October through May.

Pete wanted to stay in, so Eve and I went out and toasted in the millennium. We toasted at one pub and while we were out on the street, on the way to another pub, we heard a different pub ring in the New Year. We grinned at each , "They really are on Irish time."

What's Irish time? It isn't. It's "ish". In Ireland, there isn't a good concept of time. And Americans either get really uptight about it, or they simply accept it. For instance, if someone tells you they'll meet you at the pub for a pint at four o'clock, they'll say four-ish, and may not get there until after five or six. But of course you're still there because people have bought you pints and you've bought them pints as well. You take turns.

I asked someone why people disregard the clock, and was given a very logical answer. In the past, whenever you went from The Republic of Ireland to Northern Ireland, there was a checkpoint you had to pass through, and it could delay you for minutes or hours. This time delay has carried over, and no one really holds you to time. They just don't stress about it—and seeing that the ages on the gravestones we read usually tended to be well over eighty, maybe the Irish have the right idea...

Contrary to popular belief, the Irish do have the right idea about food. Avril and Peter had me at their home for spicy dinners a few times and I had them over for heated meals as well. Spicy isn't the norm in Ireland, so we quite enjoyed the opportunity to burn each out in the taste bud department. But besides the burn factor, those two created fabulous meals that we devoured at their beautiful old home. We'd joke about their house that they called "The Refrigerator". It was always so cold and damp in most of the house, but being in the living room, curled up by the fire, with a glass of wine in hand and traditional Irish music surrounding you, tended to make one forget the rest of the house (and world for that matter). We'd always have a fantastically fun evening together with laughter, eating, more laughter and enjoying each 's company.

Sometimes Avril and I even went to the big city and goofed around there. It was so wonderful to have a girlfriend in Greenane. We'd go shopping or touring around the area and she'd educate me about it and I could talk to her about my rollercoaster of emotions. And when the three of us were together, Peter, with his quick sense of humor, would pick up on something stupid I had said, and we'd be rolling in the aisles. Oh the wrinkles and laugh lines that can be blamed on those two.

And those two had some very entertaining friends. Patrick and Colleen had us over for a very elegant restaurant-quality dinner and side-splitting laughs one winter evening. I kept telling Colleen that she should have her own restaurant, but she kept saying how she wasn't good enough. But maybe when I "finger licked" the dessert dish, she got a clue that she really was that good. "Augh go on..." she'd say, laughing as she'd disappear into the kitchen only to bring out yet another delectable dish.

I don't understand how people who visit Ireland can say that the food isn't very good, because I sure ate like a queen while living there. Maybe most people don't get as lucky and meet such incredible cooks.

A study said that laughter is good not only for the soul, but it can possibly help prolong life. Well, judging from the fact that the Irish can drink like fish and smoke like fires, but still live to the ripe old ages of eighties and nineties, it must be true. Colleen told of a time when she was talking to a man that ended up not being the nicest of people. She told him, "If I wanted to listen to an arsehole I would have farted meself!"

The lifestyle of those funny and friendly folks was one I adjusted to quite easily, and I still find myself thinking about them and Ireland a lot: the sea and the boats, time spent on a few farms, and the cute youngsters who toured me around their dads' places. Dylan showed me their miniature Shetland ponies, and Brian showed me a bunch of calves on chains in shelters like big dogs. Brian explained that dairy calves have to be separated from their moms very early and have to be sheltered against the cold, and not left out in the fields, or they will die. I watched his dad milk the cows in a parlor identical to what I had seen when I was in New Zealand, and we talked about the milk business. The whole dairy industry is very different from the American system. The number of producers you can have is limited, depending on certain variables like area of the country in which you live or quotas available for milk production. So being a motivated entrepreneur isn't always the best thing in the milk business; you'd be limited in your growth. And their dairy products are very different from ours too. Very creamy, very rich, delicious and inexpensive.

Expensive, however, is the word I'd use to describe the five-million-dollar boat that showed up on my second to last night in Greenane. It was piloted in from Spain and practically the whole town was at the pier for the welcoming at two o'clock-ish in the morning. Fireworks, horns, the whole nine yards. The boat was beautiful. It was massive and smelled of paint and stainless steel- newness oozing out all over. Dylan gave me a tour while I said hi to all the folks I knew aboard who were there admiring this beauty. It was a very big event for the village and it was great that everyone shared in the excitement; apparently the celebration lasted until seven in the morning. Ah small towns...

A whole book about the people and times of Greenane could be written, but that's not the purpose of this story about Jesse. I just thought it might be interesting to intertwine the story of how I came to finally write the story about Jesse, with the story about Jesse. I could go on forever, talking about Joseph and Eileen and their five—no six—children (she was due the day I left), or John and Carol and singing in Clancy's Pub many Friday nights until three in the morning, or all the folks I met in O'Connors's, or Fiona, my internet pal (where I went to e-mail everyone), or Evan the milkman (yes they still deliver milk over there), or Margaret and Eric, the owners of Kearnan's, or Michael the Floridian and Kevin the guy from Wisconsin—who are both fishermen now. Or how I flew to Chicago one weekend for a wedding and the Superbowl (the townsfolk thought I was really crazy then), but that's another story entirely. The list goes on and on...I had quite the interesting three months while I was there, but enough about that.

I was very sad when I left Greenane (once again on a full moon) but I knew I'd be back someday in the not-too-distant future. I had semi-accomplished my goals by almost finishing my book, spending time in a country I love and spending time with a man who had captured my heart. I realized that there could never be a sound relationship between us—he had his life, I had mine and indeed they were very different. But now I wouldn't go back to Colorado pining away for an Irish fisherman; I just know that I'll never forget him. I think about Danny and sigh with happiness when I remember his mannerisms, his eyes, his heart that touched mine and his wonderful smile. I try to be content in having had the experience of meeting and knowing him, which resulted in a chance for me to live in Ireland. So it didn't end up quite like a romance novel, but this was real life and besides, I'm sure that I will run into him again, someday...

Chapter 43

That someday always comes when you're a pet owner. The day your beloved friend goes downhill. Hopefully it happens quickly so neither of you suffer. Well, I was lucky with Jesse. That last summer, she had a problem with her ears and it caused her to go "out of balance", but she wasn't in pain and she never hurt herself. She just sometimes walked as if she had been to an Irish pub. She padded along sideways with her head tilted to one side, and she looked funny, but she didn't have that silly Irish grin while she was concentrating on staying upright.

I subconsciously knew her time with me was coming to an end. She was going to be fourteen that fall. She was an old dog now, and it had been a few years since I had taken her on any big trips. She just couldn't travel the long distances anymore so I always made sure that when I had to go, I packed my things out of her sight, since she used to get so excited when she saw the big red suitcase on the bed.

So instead, we went on short camping trips, which she loved and could still endure. She had always enjoyed being in camp mode even if it was a little hard on her. She'd try to sleep during the day because she guarded me at night; quietly sitting by the fire all night long. Of course she always tried to do this without me realizing it, never wanting me to think she was being a real dog, but I guess she never could fight those instincts. We had some great times those last months while camping in the mountains and spending fun times together. My sister's family and my brother Dave were also able to enjoy her company while out camping that last summer.

But then, one evening in August when I was sitting watching TV, she walked over to the corner of the room and stood with her head deep in the corner. I called to her, but she didn't move. I walked over to her and seemed to have scared her. She started to do this strange corner-staring thing a few times and I knew something was wrong. Another time she went into the garbage when I was standing right there and she had never done that—the garbage event had always been a home-alone activity.

Now it was beginning to be apparent that her hearing was going. One day I walked into the house to find a small chipmunk sitting next to her, chatting away, as she snoozed. Jesse was totally oblivious to the noisy critter. Other times I'd come home and think she was dead. I'd call loudly to her and she didn't move. It'd give me a heart attack. I'd run up to her and touch her and she always woke up. But even though her hearing was going, she was healthy and happy and still ran around in the yard and played.

However on Labor Day weekend that year, she started a whole new behavior. She'd look at me, and her head would shake subtly, but very rapidly. I called the vet and he said to bring her in on Tuesday. Tom did a full blood work up on her and said he'd call me later on Wednesday, but he gave me some pills to give her on Thursday morning (depending on the results from Wednesday). His report was that she was in excellent shape as far as her organs were concerned, but it seemed that her brain was not quite right. From what I had told him, and when he saw her "corner staring" in his office, he knew something was wrong. He had been her vet for years and had never seen her act like this.

I gave her a pill on Thursday morning after breakfast and let her out. When I went to let her back inside, she was gone. Trying not to worry, and thinking she was out carousing, I ran some errands—expecting her to be home as usual when I returned. She wasn't. Now I was worried. In her old age, she didn't stay gone this long anymore. I called B and we decided to get the horses and go out looking for her. We spent hours riding all around the mountain looking for Jesse and intermittently going home to check my answering machine for any messages about her. Finally in the afternoon, there was a message from a lady who had her down the mountain. We raced down and found them. I was so happy to have her back, but when I talked to her, she acted like she didn't know who I was. This wasn't like Jesse at all. I took her home and settled her in before I headed to work.

When I returned home, I found Jesse by the door. She was spinning in circles on the carpet with her front legs. Her back legs had gone out on her, yet she was still trying to move around. Furniture was knocked over, plants were spilled, chairs were moved out from the wall—the house was a mess. She had apparently been in turmoil for a while. I was heartbroken at the thought. I tried to help her stand to no avail, and then tried to calm her down while I called B and asked her what I should do. She said to call Tom, despite the late hour and see what he said. So I called him, told him what was happening, and asked him if it was because of the pill. He said probably not, but that I should wait and see how she was in the morning, just in case. I was able to calm Jesse down, and sat on the living room floor with her all through the night.

She lay against my left leg as I leaned against the couch and she put her head on my right thigh. I stroked the soft fur as I talked quietly to my friend of fourteen years. She didn't move while she slept on me as I constantly petted her, but at one point, she slowly moved her head and looked up at me. She really looked into my eyes, and sighed a very heavy sigh. I knew in my heart that she was telling me that it was time for me to let her go, and it was fine with her. I was in constant tears while I was trying to hang on to what I knew was my last time with Jesse.

Around five o'clock a.m., she struggled to get up, but fell over again and again, and I couldn't make her stay still. From the way she looked at me and fought my attempts to quiet and calm her down, I knew she was miserable. So, true to the promise I had made to her all those years ago—that I would never let her suffer—I called Tom and told him that I had to bring her in right away. I woke up my housemate Mark and he drove us there, while I held Jesse and tried to calm her down.

She sat quietly on the sidewalk for a moment while we waited for Tom to open the door, but then she tried to walk, and because she couldn't move her back legs she started to spin. I really believe she had a stroke, and except for the moment when she so clearly told me that she was ready to go, she wasn't really Jesse anymore. We carried her in and carefully placed her on the table. Tom looked at her, asked me a few questions and agreed that it was best to let her go. He prepared everything and was ready, but I wasn't, so he let me pet Jesse for a while and say goodbye to her through my tears. As I looked into Jesse's soft and beautiful retriever eyes, and kissed her on the forehead as I always did, she blankly looked back at me. My best friend with whom I had spent so many years, so many laughs, and so many wonderful memories was already gone.

I knew I was making the right decision.

But my heart was broken. I loved her so much. I wanted Jesse back.

Yet I wasn't going to put her through any testing or probing to try to save her, just so I might get a few more months out of her. I made a promise to her when she was 5 weeks old, she already told me that she was ready to leave, and I was going to honor her will—despite my incredible sorrow.

Tom had red-rimmed eyes as he gave her the injection that sent her on her way and I watched her slip peacefully into an eternal sleep. I couldn't stop petting her beautiful soft white coat of fur even after Tom told me that she was gone. I looked down at the body of my wonderful dog and was overtaken with emotion. I would never see her silly expressions, hear her goofy barks, enjoy the mountains with her, or discover that she had eaten her beloved bread again.

It was the saddest moment of my life.

I had planned to go horse camping that weekend, but when Jesse got sick, it depended on her situation. Now that she was gone, I needed to go. I had to have a few days to digest the fact that Jesse was no longer with me, and going away would help. I could not even think about being home alone all weekend without Jesse.

I asked Tom about burying her because I wasn't sure of the laws of the county. He told me that it was fine but she had to be down about five to six feet deep if I was going to bury her on the mountain. That way none of the wildlife would get at her. I told him I didn't know what to do because I didn't have the strength to do it right then. I think Tom knew how over-whelmed with sorrow I was and he suggested that I leave her with him for the weekend and get her on Monday. I was relieved and thanked him for doing that for me.

Mark and I headed home while the rising sun was making an appearance over the Continental Divide and painting the sky with a soft pink glow. When we reached the house, I was amazed to find an incredible feeling of peace filling my being. Jesse was fine now. I had not let my friend down, no matter how much it hurt me. It had been the right choice.

I went inside and tried to sleep. I was exhausted on all counts. I called my friend whom I was supposed to go camping with and told him of the mornings' activities. He was sorry about Jesse and said I could meet him later than planned.

Bandit had been living with us for a while and I let her inside the house for the very first time. I needed some link to Jesse around me and Bandit was perfectly happy to oblige as she lay on my bed while I packed.

Horse camping was a good thing to be doing to keep my mind off Jesse, but I was always at the back as I was in tears pretty much the whole time. I tried to be strong, but my friends understood. They were all animal lovers too. I came home very late on Sunday night. I knew I was stalling, because I could hardly bear being in the house without Jesse. So I wasn't. I slept on the couch in the boys' living room and Kenya was at my side the whole night. She knew.

Monday morning, September 9th, arrived to reveal a glorious sunny day. I went to get B and she showed me the cross she had made. It said; "Patti's Friend Jesse" and had her birth and death dates burned into the wood. It was beautiful and we cried together about losing Jesse, then we went to pick her up from the vet's. B and I headed up the hill while Jesse bounced around in the back of the truck. I hollered to her, "Hey! Jesse! Keep it down back there!" We were feeling like Guido and Louie with a body in the black bag and I was trying to lessen my sadness with humor; didn't work.

Kim met us at the house and we were equipped with shovels, pick axes, beer and Bailey's—it was going to be an Irish funeral for my pal. We knew we had to dig a very large and deep hole for Jesse and planned on a big digging project, so we were ready. One thing about Ptarmigan Mountain... it's in the Rockies. Anyone who has ever dug a hole for fences or hitchin' rails, or any hole in the Rockies knows why they are called the Rocky Mountains. It's pretty obvious.

Well, I guess Irish luck was with us that day because even though we planned on an all day event, it took us only about a half an hour to dig the six foot long by five foot wide by five foot deep grave. We were stunned. We didn't even hit a fist sized rock. It truly was the perfect spot that B had chosen for Jesse's grave.

I asked B and Kim to take Jesse out of the bag for me because I didn't want to see her until I knew that she looked OK, so to speak. I wouldn't have been able to deal with anything gross. As I was slowly and carefully wrapping her in her blanket, petting the beautiful soft white fur for the last time, barely seeing through the tears that were steadily streaming down my face, Kenya came over to sniff the frozen shell that was my friend. I yelled at her to go away, but she ignored me and curiously smelled Jesse's body, then she emitted a soft whimper. She looked at me, then slowly turned and walked away. She knew.

Kim handed me a beer, I said thanks, cracked it open and managed to sip it before Kim laughed, "That was for Jesse!"

Oops. Well there was more. I wanted to bury her with her blanket, a beer and her collar. Not that I believe she'd need any of them where she was (I don't think they allow beer over the Rainbow Bridge) but... I just wanted to do this. "The Legend of the Rainbow Bridge" is a marvelous poem about what happens to your pet when they die, and it's included later.

So, after carefully placing Jesse and her things into the massive hole in the ground, we gently covered her with dirt, and then piled rocks over the grave to deter any animals from disturbing her final resting place. We planted some flowers that B bought and I said my final goodbye to her. As we looked down at the perfect spot where her body would spend eternity, I was overcome with sorrow that she was really gone. I was going to miss Jesse so much, but on that day, even though I was missing her, I was at peace with the fact that she had a wonderful life, a relatively quick death, and a great funeral on a beautiful sunny day in the Rocky Mountains, where she had spent a major part of that long and happy life.

We decided to go to lunch because now we had the time, since the dreaded digging project ended up being a quick and easy chore. When I drove down the hill, Kenya followed my truck. It was the only time that she ever did. She absolutely would not go home, so I put her in the cab with me and we headed down the mountain. She stayed in the cab during lunch, but jumped through the window into the bed, after lunch, when I stopped to see Carolyn—who had just returned from burying her father in Minnesota.

I went up the stairs to the office where Carolyn worked and found her standing at the file cabinet and gave her a hug.

"Hey Carolyn. How're you doing?"

"Well, I'm OK. I guess."

"How's your mom doing with all this?"

"She'll be alright. You know Maxine."

"Yeah."

"How's Jesse doing?" Carolyn knew that Jesse wasn't well because she had called the week before to tell me about Ed.

"I just buried her." I told Carolyn, as I broke out into tears.

"Oh Patti. I'm so sorry."

Now we were both crying, so we decided to go have a beer at The Old Dillon Inn. While we were sitting at the bar, talking about death and funerals, there was a commotion at the front door and Kenya blasted in, ran to my stool and lay down at my feet. Since all the staff knew what Carolyn and I were going through, no one said a word about Kenya. Understand that I'm not comparing losing an animal to losing your father, but we were both emotionally wrecked.

When it was time to go, the three of us walked together and when we opened the door of the dark bar to peer out into the bright sunlight, I looked up at my house and was breathless. Arching high up above our house on the mountainside was one of the brightest and most beautiful rainbows I had ever seen. And the left side, where you would look for the pot of gold, was directly over the spot where Jesse was buried. It was an awesome sight and sent me into tears all over again.

Jesse really was over The Rainbow Bridge and someone was telling me that she was doing fine. I knew then, that I would be too.

The Legend of the Rainbow Bridge

There is a bridge connecting Heaven and Earth. It is called the Rainbow Bridge because of its many colors.

Just this side of The Rainbow Bridge is a land of meadows, hills and valleys with lush green grass. When a beloved pet dies, they go to this place. There is always food and water and warm spring weather. The old and frail animals are young again. Those who are maimed are made whole again. They play all day with each .

There is only one thing missing. They are not with their special person who loved them on Earth.

So, each day they run and play until the day comes when one suddenly stops playing and looks up! The nose twitches! The ears are up! The eyes are staring! And this one suddenly runs from the group. You have been seen! And when you and your special friend meet, you take him or her in your arms and embrace. Your face is kissed again and again, and you look once more into the eyes of your beloved friend.

Then you cross the Rainbow Bridge together, never again to be separated.

Author Unknown

This is the obituary I sent out to Jesse's friends—dog and human.

Born: October 28, 1982
Died: September 6, 1996

Beloved friend and greatest companion a person could have. Jesse was born in Nashville, Tn. and moved to Frisco, Co. at the age of five, where she hiked, camped, chased chipmunks and made new friends. She moved to Pennsylvania for a brief period of country living before going on to Illinois for a time of family life.

At the age of nine, she returned to Colorado to resume her favorite past-times and make some new friends. She traveled extensively over the United States, as well as Canada and Alaska- making friends wherever she went. It was her face that made her way.

In the fall of her thirteenth year, she moved to the top of the mountain to live out the remainder of her life in great happiness and freedom. She will be missed and remembered with great love and wonderful memories.

She is survived by: Sasha, Raleigh, Tressie, Hannah, Sophie, Indigo, Le Roy, Kenya, Rusty, Peejo, Pebbles, Maya, Friskie, Patch, Jubilee, Louie, Keesha, and Bandit.

Services were on September 9, with an unprecedented rock-less ceremony and an incredibly beautiful rainbow.

Maybe now that this project is finished, I'm ready to get another dog. But first I suppose I need to find a new place to live and get a job. I have followed my heart, lived a dream and now I need to "get on with my life". It's a strange feeling to be so unsettled. Sense of belonging and identity are hard to have when you're in the middle of a crossroads, but I'm figuring it out.

Even though our American culture doesn't encourage us to step back and look at our lives—because we are so wrapped up in too many things—I am lucky that I have been able to step back.

Living in Ireland has opened my eyes to the possibility that the Irish have the right idea about a few things. Many of the people I met lead simple lives, are easily entertained, laugh a lot, and are very content. No, they are not always drunk—as some of my friends laughingly suggest—although they love their Guinness and I can't blame them a bit. Sure technology is catching up there; everyone has a mobile phone it seems, and this new thing called texting is outrageous. They'll be sitting at the bar and texting a joke to the guy sitting next to them! But they still value family, friends and relationships a great deal, as opposed to who has the most toys or the biggest house.

I'm not really into material things and never have wanted a career—even though I was trained for one—and I have always wondered, "What's wrong with me? Why do I just want a simple life? Why am I this way?" Well, on that last day in Ireland, I had a revelation. I figured it out. It's just my nature. It's just the way I am and that's fine. I don't have to feel like an unsuccessful person because I don't have all the things that most Americans judge one to have to have to be successful.

Happiness equals success...right?

I have always joked that I was born one hundred years too late and was different, but now I know that's OK. Ireland helped me to realize this in a wonderful way. I'm happy with my simple, yet exciting life, and that's all that matters.

I re-read the book, "Tuesdays With Morrie" and found that even though I enjoyed it the first time around, it had a profound effect on me the second time I read it. I recommend it to anyone sitting in a crossroad. It can help, really.

The Last Word...

Well, I've completed reviewing this book and know that I have left out many stories: like when Jesse picked up a sausage but then dropped it for the loaf of bread at an abandoned cabin in the mountains, or how she tried to drown my brother Rick, or how her lip always caught on her tooth—a very funny expression, or when she shredded Wendy's fence (along with the screen that I mentioned) to get into the front yard, or when I was in Scotland trying to decide if it really was the time to write a book about Jesse—when a German shepherd appeared out of nowhere. Lots of stories, but I had to pick and choose. And reading the last part of this book was extremely difficult. Every, single, time.

Well, I've figured out what I'm going to do. I'm leaving the Colorado Mountains where I have achieved one of my childhood dreams: to live in a small cabin in the mountains, have a horse and ride and enjoy the beautiful mountains.

Now I'm ready to try to reach another dream: to live in an old white country farm house with a wonderful porch, a huge garden with home grown tomatoes, and my horse out back. So, I'm moving to Wisconsin (to be closer to my family) where I hope this dream comes true. Of course I'm waiting for my favorite season, autumn, so I can make the transition as positive as possible.

I have always tried to learn to fertilize my own grass, so it isn't greener on the side.

So now it's on to fertilizing whatever new grass I find to live on, and maybe, just maybe, it will always be green, green, Irish green...

About the Author

Patti lives in High River, Alberta Canada with her horse Jimmy. She remains dog-less but plans to eventually share life with another dog.

Because she lived in Ireland while writing this book, she wrote under the name of her birth father who died when she was one and a half years old. He was pure Irish and she wanted to honour her heritage.

Her adopted name is DiVita, which is the name she lives with, and is the name on the restaurant movie that interrupted this book project 15 years ago. _"Did I Say Thousand Island?"_ was premiered in 2007 and has been well received in over 211 countries so far. (She went back to Ireland in 2003 to write her movie, but not to the same village...)

Patti has been instrumental in raising awareness and funds regarding the Global Water Crisis through her movie. Proceeds from this book have paid for a well in Cambodia. Future donations will go to the SPCA- Society for the Prevention of Cruelty to Animals.

All photos in this book were taken by the author except:

pg.   90   taken by Joyce Smith
pg. 248   taken by B Casapulla
pg. 234   taken by High Country Vet Clinic

If you enjoyed this book, I would greatly appreciate it if you would put a review on Amazon.

Thank you for your help, Patti

Peace...

www.ingramcontent.com/pod-product-compliance
Lightning Source LLC
Chambersburg PA
CBHW031828090426

42741CB00005B/163